VOICES OF ARABIA

VOICES OF
ARABIA

A Collection of the Poetry of Place

Selected, introduced and translated by
T. J. GORTON

ELAND • LONDON

First published in October 2009 by Eland Publishing Ltd,
61 Exmouth Market, Clerkenwell, London EC1R 4QL

This arrangement, commentary and
translations © T. J. Gorton

ISBN   978 1 906011 20 8

Pages designed and typeset by Antony Gray
Cover image:
Detail of *Market Place Outside the Gates of Cairo* 1878
copyright © Österreichische Galerie,
Belvedere, Vienna, Austria
Printed and bound in Spain by
GraphyCems, Navarra

CONTENTS

INTRODUCTION

THE ORIGINS OF ARABIC POETRY

As with many interesting subjects about which very little is known for sure, the origin of Arabic poetry has given rise to a lot of speculation. What we actually know is limited to this: beginning in about the eighth century AD, Muslims began to compile and comment in writing on the text of the Holy Quran, and this process favoured the written compilation of what were then considered to be the monuments of Arabic poetry from the Time of Ignorance (possibly better translated 'Wildness'), that is, from before the revelation of the Holy Quran to the Prophet Muhammad. From the complex metres and forms of these earliest recorded poems, it is clear that there was a flourishing poetic art among the tribes living in and near the Arabian Peninsula who spoke the Semitic language we call Arabic, in all likelihood by the early sixth century AD. This poetry must have been passed on by memory from one generation to another; some of it could have been composed through oral improvisation – indeed, metrically interchangeable formulaic phrases have been identified in pre-Islamic poetry, just as in Homer. But here we stray into speculation.

These poems, whatever their origin, were so revered by the Arabs that seven of them – as the story goes – were chosen to be suspended in the Holy of Holies, the Ka'ba at Mecca in the pre-Islamic period. There is actually no evidence that they were suspended anywhere or even written down at all before the

Hegira, nor that they were selected as a discrete group of seven before the late ninth century AD; but they did come over time to be revered as the seminal masterpieces of the language, despite their pagan origin. Many of the thematic and metrical conventions observed in those *qasida*s or 'odes' continued to provide the canon for Arabic poetry until modern times, an astounding example of formal continuity even if the inspiration of the later practitioners was not comparable to that of their desert-dwelling models.

One thing that is not open to argument is the importance, perhaps the unique importance, of poetry in Arabian life around the time of the first extant poems in the language. In the much-quoted words of an eleventh-century Arab, Ibn Rashiq:

> When there appeared a poet in a family of the Arabs, the other tribes round about would gather together to that family and wish them joy of their good luck. Feasts would be got ready, the women of the tribe would join together in bands, playing upon lutes, as they were wont to do at bridals, and the men and boys would congratulate one another; for a poet was a defence to the honour of them all, a weapon to ward off insult from their good name, and a means of perpetuating their glorious deeds and of establishing their fame for ever. And they used not to wish one another joy but for three things – the birth of a boy, the coming to light of a poet, and the foaling of a noble mare.[1]

---

[1] Sir Charles Lyall, *Ancient Arabian Poetry* (London, 1930), p. 17.

THE *QASIDA*

The poetic tradition that appears so suddenly is an astonishingly mature one: serious poetry consisting of long (often over 100 lines) monorhyme pieces with a set thematic progression: the poet weeps over an abandoned campsite in the desert, addressing his companions (usually in the number of two) with his '*ubi sunt*', then progresses to an amorous poem (also elegiac), the *nasib*; then describes his own prowess in warfare (*fakhr* or *hamasa*), and finally the point (*gharad*) of it all, usually the *madih* or praise of the person to whom the poem is addressed. Anything shorter or lacking any of the set components is a *qit'a* or 'fragment'. This might sound formulaic: but good poets have always used tight formal constraints to shine through nuance. One of them said so (literal translation):

> My fellow tribesmen saw how I aspired to do great things,
>   and tried to imitate me,
> But their efforts were laboured, their souls constrained *as*
>   *poetry is by metre* [2]

The problem, of course, is that the canon outlived itself, and there are certainly tiresome poems where an urban poet who has obviously never seen the desert or a camel weeps over the campsite and goes through the whole routine in a panegyric to another city-dweller who never left Cairo or Seville or Baghdad in his life. But, especially prior to about 1000 AD, the best poets wrote intensely personal, highly irreverent and often licentious verse that would have got a contemporary Western European burned at the stake.

[2] Abu Firas, *Diwan Abi Firas*, ed. Al-Husain bin Khalawaih (Beirut, 1966), p.178.

The story goes that a student in a French language class, on hearing '*Pierre qui roule n'amasse pas mousse*', exclaimed, 'How beautiful!' There is even more danger of this in a language which is more exotic for the Western reader than French; the following are a few of the stock images which the poets embroider on, the embroidery being the point, not the image itself (a distinction already pithily made by a pre-Islamic poet):

> Have the poets left a single spot where a patch can still be sewed?

Take 'heat and water/passion and tears'. This image is taken as a given and endlessly reworked:

> Coursing tears and burning breast
> Water and fire
> Only joined by momentous events

Others include the lightning smile of the beloved, the lover who grows so thin through yearning that the wind blows him away, the eyes like bows shooting glances like arrows, the river's surface rippling like chain-mail, and so on. Sometimes the reader's knowledge and expectation of a stock image is taken for granted, and the reference is often oblique, playful or ironic.

The rhetorical devices used by poets were exhaustively described by Arab critics from an early time; while some are common to most poetics (*tibaq*, antithesis or mentioning two words of opposite meaning in the same line), or *mubalagha* (hyperbole), some are peculiar to Arabic (*jinas*, the juxtaposing of two words having the same trilateral root consonants, but different meanings, especially the variant *jinas musahhaf*, where the words differ in their diacritical markings, i.e. the shape of the letters without the single dot that distinguishes '*ra*'' from '*za*'', for instance). This gets very recondite for the non-Arabist, and as a result some highly praised poems seem to an outsider to be merely sterile exercises in accumulating rhetorical figures.

ARABIC METRE

Arabic metrics are quantitative, based on the patterns of long and short vowels, and could be illustrated by musical notation as easily as any other. That may explain why so much of Arabic poetry was intended to be sung, or was later set to music. There are theories that the system used to classify the numerous and varied metres was derived from the beating of copper in the bazaar, or the different gaits of the camel; but what is certain is that Arabic poetry is built on a rhythmic basis of great variety and subtlety. There is a metre for high-falutin' encomia (*tawil*), one (*rajaz*, the oldest) for narrative verse and doggerel, and many others for lyrical or elegiac verse. Their metres are defined by the juxtaposition of short and long syllables, rather than with stress in the spoken language (though a long and normally stressed syllable may, and often do, coincide). I will try to illustrate.

Tawil ('long') is the solemn *grand chant* metre of the Arabs. If you tried to duplicate its powerful, swelling, hypnotic rhythm in English you might get something like

Aríse now, take úp your swórd and gírd ón your báttle-géar

Contrast this with the tripping rhythm of *kamil* ('complete'), the metre of 'Antara's *mu'allaqa*:

Little bóys and bíg ónes pláy at wár in the súmmertíme

There are just enough permitted variations in the metres that,

11

once a given form is chosen, it governs every line in a long poem without monotony; in Arabic, metre and language are tightly woven and the result, in the best poems, is astoundingly effective at conveying a mood, a vivid image whether sadly lyrical, boisterously celebratory or ominously warlike.

THE DECLINE

After the time of al-Hallaj and al-Mutanabbi, about the turn of the Gregorian millennium, Arabic culture in general began its decline into the long dark centuries known in Arab histories as *'asr al-inhitat*, the 'age of decadence'. The Seljuk, then Mongol, invasions would soon destroy Baghdad's legendary intellectual glory; the Crusades would for a time upset the political balance in the Levant, and by the time the Renaissance came to Europe, the long Ottoman centuries had begun in the East and the *Reconquista* and Inquisition had destroyed the rich Muslim and Jewish civilizations of Iberia.

THE SELECTION

This anthology does not pretend to be a truly representative selection of Arabic verse from its origins to its decadence. I have chosen poems that I thought would be likely to interest a Western reader by virtue of their content, since that is about all one can realistically hope will survive the distortion of translation. This criterion leaves out some important poems that one would have doubtless included in an anthology intended for an Arabic-reading public, on the basis of linguistic or prosodic virtuosity.

In selecting poets for inclusion, I have gone a bit heavier on those who seem, at least, to be sharing personal emotions or experiences with us, than those whose art is more lapidary; that is a matter of personal preference and one of the prerogatives of the anthologist. There are no poems from Muslim Spain as they have been the subject of a separate anthology in this series.[3]

A Note on the Translation

What does it mean to 'translate poetry'? I am still not sure; all too aware that what I have produced is not poetry, I think I can defend the fact that it conveys in English most of the main literal meaning of the original. I have wanted to convey also some feeling for the spirit, the mood, the tone or whatever one might call it; and wherever I could, some distant approximation of the rhythm of this most musical of languages.

3 *Andalus: Moorish Songs of Love and Wine* (London: Eland, 2007).

THE POETRY

PRE-ISLAMIC

The earliest *qasida*s are important not just in themselves, but as records of the language as it existed around the time of the Quran; they have been used to explain obscure passages and vocabulary in the Holy Book itself. The beduin whose language is closest to that recorded in the ancient Odes were considered to be the guardians of the best Arabic, and for that reason it was considered part of a young man's education to spend a year with a beduin tribe, even as late as Mutanabbi in the tenth century AD (which did not prevent him from being murdered much later by beduin robbers). It takes a lot of dedication and patience for a non-Arab to enjoy the long descriptive passages about camels and desert travel, and I have favoured poems where more space is devoted to human life and passions. Most of the poets whose work has survived are *mukhadrim*, that is, born before the advent of Islam but living through it and, mostly, becoming Muslim, and this transition can be felt in some of their verse.

The Vagabonds

One of the most curious and endearing (from a safe distance) aspects of pre-Islamic poetry is the small group of poets known as *Sa'aliq* (sing. *Su'luq*), the 'outcasts' or 'vagabonds'. At a time when tribal affiliation was all-important, these men rejected their own kind and took off alone into the desert, sometimes siding with an enemy clan in the incessant warfare between neighbouring tribes. Their poetry tells of their defiance and free-spirited life, and thus avoids cliché and provides what seem to be personal vignettes from the lives of these outcasts.

Ash-Shanfara

Ash-Shanfara was one of the two most famous of the *Sa'aliq*; his *lamiyyat al-'arab* ('The Arabs', an ode rhymed on the letter *'lam'*) is considered one of the greatest poems in the language. The medieval commentaries with their *horror vacui* give numerous colourful anecdotes and details about him, but we actually know next to nothing believable about his origins or his life. The poem itself was, as we have seen, transmitted orally for two centuries before being written down, so the text is certain to contain later additions or errors. With all that, the flavour is so pungent, the story so lifelike and the language so taut, that it feels authentic.

Get your camels up and moving, men of my mother's tribe –
For I'm inclined to cast my lot with better folk than you.

Everything's packed and ready, the moon shines bright tonight;
The camels, baggage loaded, stand ready for the ride.

There has to be a place on earth where a noble man is safe,
A place where such a one finds a refuge from abuse –

I swear this land is vast and can't constrain a man
Who roves for gain or safety, if he but has his wits.

Far from you, I'll make new friends: the swiftly-trotting wolf,
Sleek and spotted panther, shaggy jackals loping by;

These are folk to trust in, you can tell your secrets to –
And they will not reject you no matter what you do.

Others may be brave enough, but when it comes to war
I'm the boldest, always first to meet the charge head-on;

And when the battle's done, the feast prepared, when greedy
      ones
Are quick to snatch the morsels – I hold my hand aloof.

That's generosity – besides, the truly chivalrous man
Makes a virtue of leaving some aside for another day.

I'm happy to do without you, since you don't give me my due,
Nor make me feel at home here; all I really need,

Are three companions: fearless heart, bright sharp sword,
And yellow, long-necked bow –

Twanging, tough but pliant, adorned with plaited thongs
Hanging down, with its leather carrying-strap:

When it lets fly an arrow, it makes a high-pitched moan – a
      screech
Like a grieving mother whose babe's been snatched away.

I'm not a thirsty one, grazing flocks when the heat dies down,
The hungry mothers' untied udders dry, leaving foals to starve;

Nor am I a coward, fearfully sticking by his wife,
Listening to her advice as to how he ought to act;

Nor yet a frightened weakling, heart fluttering up
And down like the skittish Mukka-bird,

17

And certainly not a lie-abed, in his tent all day
Oiling hair and body, rimming eyes with antimony!

Nor an unarmed, wretched good-for-nothing,
Who jumps if you say 'boo!'

Pitch-darkness does not faze me, when suddenly at night
Up looms a trackless wasteland, baffling even my strong mount.

Over hard and flinty ground we run, striking sparks and
Scattering pebbles with every beat of her four pads,

Turning my face from the slightest thought of food,
Ignoring the pangs of hunger – till *it* wastes away and dies!

I'd sooner lick dust from the ground, than let any man alive
Boast that I was in his debt or owed him the slightest thing –

Not that I couldn't have had the best you can eat or drink
And thrive on – but I couldn't take the shame:

My rebel nature goads me onward at the least affront;
I must be freely on the move, with all that that entails[4] .

I tie my guts 'round hunger as a rope-maker ties his threads
Twisting left and twisting right, until the twine is tight.

All morning I ride with no more food than the agile, ash-grey wolf,
As he lopes from one bare stretch of desert to the next.

In the morning he trots out hungry, nose into the wind
Darting to the bottom of ravines, then clambering out;

---

[4] Many lines of this poem are in such archaic language that there are
    several ways to read them; here, the poet seems to follow up on the
    statement in the preceding line that he could have had luxuries, but
    for the shame (of staying in one place).

And if he spies a prey, he turns aside to chase,
And howls a call for help: scrawny cousins soon call back,

Emaciated, muzzles grizzled, thin as arrow-shafts
Which a gambling-dealer shuffles in his palms;

Scrambling like a swarm of bees, when a honey-thief
Jabs his crooked stick down into their hive:

The wolves' jaws gape wide, as does a stump
Split by an axe, so grim and fierce they are.

One howls, the rest howl back across the open plain –
A sound like mourning women's wails wafting down to us.

They, like him, bear misfortune with a wink, wretches[5]
They no less than he, and this consoles them all;

If he complains, they do as well, but then leave off complaining,
For if complaints can do no good, you might as well forbear.

So each turns back, and runs headlong his way
Bearing as best he can his hidden sorrows' pain.

The dusky sand-grouse drinks the water I leave behind –
After searching through the night with throbbing wings;

I raced the birds to water, skirts tucked up, but not exerting
        much –
For all their beating wings, I was the first to drink!

Then I left them to it, scurrying down to the water-hole,
Bending down their crops at the edge, throats brushing water –

---

5 Literally, 'a traveller whose provisions are exhausted'.

Making such a racket, like a crowd of motley Bedu
Shouting as they pitch their camp, their day of travel done.

The grouse come from different places, drawn to the water-hole
As camels are, after a day of grazing on their own;

They don't linger sipping, but gulp their drink and go.
Like a travelling-party setting off from Uhaza in the dawn.

I'm used to lie on the hard earth's face, when at last it's time
        to sleep
My bony backbone's ridges showing through, as I curl up

With my forearm as a pillow on which to rest my head –
As knobbly as the bones a gambler throws for dice.

Shanfara seems out of favour with Lady War just now,
But for the longest time she smiled upon him;

Brought low by sinful strokes, I'm like the hunters' prey –
They've already drawn straws to share my meat!

And while I sleep, so do they, but with their eyes wide open,
Hastening towards my resting-place, bringing direst death.

Worries are my companions, who visit me as often
As a recurring fever, and are heavier to bear;

When they show up, I fight them off – but then
They come at me again, from down below, or else from up above.

And if you see me striding out in the hottest midday sun,
Shoeless, barefoot and wretched as a snake[6]

---

[6] There is some controversy as to the meaning of this word, literally 'daughter of the sand', which could mean 'oryx' or 'snake'. Both animals had a reputation for going out in the midday sun.

Well, resolve does me for sandals, and for clothes
I wear patient endurance on a heart like a desert cat's.

I've known poverty, and riches in my time: true riches are attained
By he who wanders far and strives, and never minds the risks.

Want never made me anxious, nor did I show off my poverty;
But neither did I flaunt my wealth, putting on boastful airs.

Nonsense never makes me lose my cool, and you won't catch me
Asking endless questions, prattling gossip for slander's sake.

I remember nights so cold and chill, a desperate bowman might
Burn his bow and arrow-shafts to keep the cold away!

On one such night I ploughed ahead through the gloom and rain,
No friends save burning hunger, bitter cold, and fearful
        shuddering;

That night I made women widows, children orphans too,
But I returned as I set out, through the night, black as black
        can be.

Next morning, at Ghumaisa in the hills, some sat and asked:
What happened, while the rest told what they knew.

One said, 'Our dogs howled in the night, and so we said –
"What is it? A wolf on the prowl, perhaps a young hyena?"

'They howled just once, then curled and slept, and so we told
        ourselves:
"Could be a startled sand-grouse, or just a fledgling hawk?"

'If a *jinn* it was, that came by night, it was a wondrous thing
but if a man – he did a deed that no man ever did.'

And I recall a Dog-day noon, when the very mirages melt
While the vipers slip and slither along the baking ground;

Ahead I went, face to sun and heat, with no veil between us,
Nothing to protect me except my tattered cloak.

On my head, a shock of hair, groomed only by the wind
Which makes the uncombed side-locks fly about.

It's been years since my hair's known greasing or delousing,
All stuck-up with dirt, unwashed this year or more.

Walking, ever crossing wind-swept deserts, flat and bare as a
    shield,
A wilderness never trodden by any two legs before mine.

I'd climb to the highest vantage-point, scanning from far to near
Standing a while to look around, then squatting on my heels.

Ibexes, brown as dust, wander about me, looking for all the
    world
Like young maidens wearing robes that trail their trains behind;

And in the heat, they lie dozing around me, as though I was
    one of them:
White leg, curved horn – ledge-stepping up the mountain to
    remote refuge.

Ta'abbata Sharran

This 'Vagabond' poet's real name was Thabit bin Jabir al-Fahmi, but he is widely known by his obscure nickname, which means literally 'he put evil under his arm'. This is usually (but unconvincingly) explained as meaning that he put his sword there as he rushed out to exact vengeance for an insult. This short *qit'a* or 'fragment' is interesting in that it illustrates the pre-Islamic belief in two kinds of supernatural creatures: *ghilan* (sing. *ghul*) and *jinn* (sing. *jinni*). The former, ghouls to us, were female (though in later literature they are more commonly male), universally sinister beings, constantly changing shape. Both could be killed by a strong and skilful man provided he did it cleanly, with one blow: a second restored them to life. As we shall see, a wounded *jinni* sometimes tricked her attackers by asking for another blow. *Jinn* were invisible most of the time, but some were friendly and poets especially were thought to have their own *jinni*, comparable to the Greek *daimon*.

Hey, who will be the messenger, who will tell the youth of Fahm
About what I met with face to face, out in Raha Bitan?

Well, it was a ghoul I ran across, darting through the desert wastes,
Flat as parchment, treeless, waterless, a bad and empty place;

So I said to her, 'We're both tired, worn out with travelling far –
It's late, so leave me be, and let me go my way.'

She rushes straight for me, to attack me viciously –
But I put out my hand, grip my polished Yemen blade,

23

Keep my wits about me, strike her on her neck and arms:
And down she falls, wounded mortally.

'Strike me again!' said she, but I answered her like this:
'Not so fast! Just keep your place, for I've a steady heart.'

I spent the night on top of her, so in the morning light
I could see just what it was I had chanced upon.

And in the dawn I saw: two eyes, in the ugliest of heads
Like a tom-cat's, but its tongue was cleft in two;

Two legs with cloven hoofs, the mangy skin of a dog –
Clothed in lowly woollen rags, or remains of water-skins.

THE *RITHA'* (or *marthiya*, pl. *marathi*),
THE LAMENT OR ELEGIAC POETRY

Among the genres of early Arabic poetry, one that stands out for its expression of powerful feelings and its sincerity is the lament. It is also a genre where women poets compete on equal footing with men. In fact there may have been a lot more poetry by women, but as few of them were lucky enough to have their works collected in a *Diwan*, most of what we have is fragments found in anthologies. The earliest poetic laments appear just before the advent of Islam, a time of incessant wars and feuds and ambushes, so there was no lack of potential subject matter. It seems to me that some of the women poets whose *marathi* have survived produced the most moving examples of the genre in world literature.

Al-Khansa'

Al-Khansa' is a nickname meaning 'snub-nosed'; her real name is Tumadir bint 'Amr. This woman poet of the Banu Sulaym tribe was born towards the end of the sixth century AD and is reported to have had a long life; many stories are told of her, most or all of which are probably fictitious. What we do know is that her full brother Mu'awiya, and then her half-brother Sakhr, were killed in battles with the arch-enemies of their tribe, the Banu Murra; she composed numerous laments for each, and several poems which were calls for vengeance for their deaths. This is one of her best-known laments for Sakhr:

All night I toss and turn, assailed by memories; while
In the morning I awake worn out by the catastrophe,

The death of Sakhr – and such a youth he was!
On the battle-day, who could parry and thrust like him?

Who but Sakhr would take arms against a stubborn foe,
To defend the right of one unfairly trodden down?

His death has been a disaster, the like I've never seen –
Not in the world of men, nor in the world of Jinn.

Steadfast against the slings and arrows of destiny,
Quick-witted, decisive, never muddled for a moment;

When times were hard for those about, he was most generous
To any who sought his help, to neighbours – or his wife;

To all those guests who knocked at night, or asked him for
        refuge –
People whose hearts were sorely frightened at the slightest sound,

He was kindness itself, taking in those desperate souls
And making sure their minds were free from care.

Oh Sakhr! Never shall I forget you, not until
I part from my very heart's blood, my shallow grave dug out.

Every time the sun comes up, I am reminded of Sakhr,
Just as I remember him with every setting sun;

If there hadn't been so many people around, weeping
For their own loved ones, I would have surely killed myself.

I can still see them before me: the mother grieving for her dead
        child,
The wife, wailing over her dead husband on that day of woe –

Both weeping for the ones they lost, on the evening of the
Very day disaster struck, or the night that followed.

Even though they did not grieve for the likes of my brother,
It consoled me to see that I am not alone in grieving so.

The day I parted from Sakhr abu Hassan, I said good-bye
To every delight or comfort I had known.

Woe is me, and woeful too our mother – Can it really be,
He spends the morning in that grave, and then the evening too?

Al-Samaw'al

Al-Samaw'al Ibn Gharid ibn 'Adiya' lived in the middle of
the sixth century AD, a member of a Jewish Arab tribe who
lived in the fortress of al-Ablaq near Taima'. His name is still
a by-word for 'faithful' (hence the proverb '[even] more
faithful than al-Samaw'al'), stemming from his alleged
sheltering of the other famous pre-Islamic poet Imru' al-
Qais, or of weapons and armour belonging to him (an
almost certainly spurious legend, despite its wide currency).
His high moral tone is certainly evident in this poem, and
his early reputation for it is clear from the piece by al-A'sha
that follows it.

If a man keeps his honour free from the slightest stain
Then any robe he cloaks himself in is beautiful to see;

If he never forces himself to endure the worst hardships
Then he will find no way to merit goodly praise.

One woman taunted us, for we were far outnumbered –
I merely said, 'Truly noble men are few'

Are they not few, those remaining who, like us
Reached the lofty peaks, young and old men too?

What does it harm us, if we be but few, so long as on our side
We have a great ally, while most men are allied with baseness?

Up on our lofty mountain,[7] those who seek refuge with us
Live safely, so high up that eyes fall back, weary with the strain;

Its base is down beneath the Earth, while its peak rises up
To the very stars, so high and unattainable it is.

And as for us, we are a folk who don't shy away from death,
The way the men of 'Amir do, or those of Salul –

Our love of dying hastens our rendezvous with Death,
While they recoil from it, and live out their lengthy lives.

No lord of our tribe ever died a natural death,
Nor lay unavenged on the spot where he was killed;

Our souls pour out on the sword-blade's edge,
And only on the sword-edge do they pour.

Our line is pure, never sullied or diluted
By the noble mares and stallions of our line –

We stand upon the best of shoulders, and when it's time
The bellies we go down on are the best!

We're as pure as the shower of rain, no bluntness in our steel,
Nor has any miser been numbered in our ranks.

---

[7] This appears to be meant both literally (al-Ablaq) and, especially, figuratively (the 'lofty peak of virtue').

We spurn if we like what other men say –
But when we speak, no man dares object.

Never did we douse our fire, hearing a night-caller knock,
Nor did a visitor ever find our welcome wanting warmth.

The battle-days we fought on have gone down in fame,
Marked out in memory like blazes on noble steeds;

Our swords are blunted, from smiting armoured warriors
In battles all over the East, still more throughout the West;

Their custom, once unsheathed, is not to be put back
Until they've spilt the blood of an armed enemy.

If our fame hasn't reached you, go and ask around
About us – and about them – for it's better to be informed;

The Banu Dayan are the pole of their people, the axle
Of their mill-stone: everything turns and revolves around them.

Maymun ibn Qays al-A'sha

From the renowned north-eastern-Arabian tribe, Qays ibn
Tha'laba, al-A'sha was a contemporary of Muhammad, a
travelling, professional poet with bad eyesight who had a
fondness for wine and women and knew so much Christian
lore that there has been informed speculation that he was,
in fact, a Christian. This poem may be a fragment of a lost,
longer ode; I have chosen it because of its vividness as well
as its reference to al-Samaw'al, who may (or may not) have
been related to the Shuraih to whom the poem is addressed.

Don't desert me O Shuraih, now that my fingers have just grasped
The ropes of your protection – having just escaped from bonds;

Far have I travelled, from Baniqya down to Aden, a long
Time of going to and fro among the foreigners.

Your sire was the most faithful of them all to his promise, the best
Of all neighbours – that's too well-known to be denied –

Generous as a rain-cloud, pouring forth on demand,
But bold as any lion in a fight, and just as fierce.

Be like Samaw'al, when the enemy army loomed
A host so large it was dark as night, and came on just as slow

If you're under the protection of Ibn Hayya, you'll find him
Truer to his promise, a better defender than Ibn 'Ammar.[8]

Samaw'al lived on Mount Ablaq in the country of Tayma',
A fortress never taken, and he a protector never false

When Harith laid it siege, he offered a choice of shames;
Samaw'al said 'I'm listening, say what you want to say.'

He said, 'Either break your promise, or I'll kill your son –
There is no happy choice in a dilemma such as this.'

Samaw'al hesitated for a second, then said to him:
'Kill your hostage, for I gave my word and bond!

If you do kill him, he's not my only son –
But you'll have killed a fine and noble boy.

Our wealth is great, our honour never stained;
His brothers are as good as him, not evil boys at all,

8 This 'plug' has lost its force, as the identity of Ibn 'Ammar is unknown.

They learned from me the code of living reasonably,
But they're no fools when War girds up its loins.

If you do harm him, others will survive me when I'm gone,
The Good Lord[9] – and pure, sinless women will see to that!

When they're at home, their talk's no idle prattle
And if I entrust my secrets to them they are safe.'

So Thabit stood there, ready to kill the boy, and said:
'Look down here, Samaw'al, you'll see the flowing blood –

Must I really kill him in cold blood? Won't you relent,
And give the things to me?' How bitter this was for Samaw'al!

And then Harith cut his throat, and Samaw'al's heart was
        filled with grief
For his son, sharp as the burning pain that's caused by fire

His choice was the suits of armour, and the promise that
        he'd made;
His word was kept, his name was not reviled.

He said, 'I will not purchase shame at the cost of my dear honour',
So he chose the honour of renown, and did not choose the shame.

The restraint he showed was the essence of the man: he was
A fire-brand of loyalty, in him its flame burned bright and true.

---

9 The word for 'lord' is *rabb*, slightly unusual for the time and context;
   possibly a reference to Samaw'al's Jewish faith?

'Antara ibn Shaddad

This (late, but not *mukhadrim*) pre-Islamic poet was said to be the son of a black slave, and thus had to struggle to become a freeman of his tribe. His legendary love for 'Abla was later woven into a cycle of romances. His most famous poem was later considered to merit inclusion in the *mu'allaqat*; it also takes up the 'nothing new under the sun/ *tout est dit*' theme with remarkable dexterity, levelling irony at the cliché of '*ubi sunt*' that traditionally started every ode.

There are other reasons for choosing this Ode. 'Antara composes in the metre *kamil*, one that permits the beginning of every (normally 4-syllable) foot to be either one long or two short syllables; in the latter case the foot has five. This makes it more varied than the more solemn metre usually reserved for major poems, *tuwil* or 'long'; a hemistich where two or more of the feet have the two-short-syllable variant is fast and tripping; one with three four-syllable feet (of which three are long) is more ponderous, giving the Arabic a wonderfully musical rhythm which a master poet like 'Antara uses to great advantage. Sadly, I am not capable of translating those subtle variations of cadence. What should come through, even in the dim mirror of translation, is 'Antara's originality of image, which sometimes carries him away. My favourite is when he starts singing the praises of his beloved's alluring mouth, comparing it to a fresh green meadow; then tells us that there is no beast there save a solitary fly (to show us how pure and clean it is); then describes the fly humming to himself; then has him rubbing one leg against the other 'like a one-armed man bent on striking fire from a flint'. By then we have forgotten about the fly, not to mention her pearly teeth, and are ourselves caught up with this one-armed flint-striker!

Have the poets left a single spot on which a patch can still be
       sewn?
Or do you really think you recognised her Dwelling by yourself?

Speak to me, Jiwa' campsite where 'Abla used to live –
'Abla's dwelling, may this morning find you safe and well
       content![10]

I stopped my good she-camel and tarried at that spot,
As though it were a castle, worth lingering at a while

'Abla and her tribe lived here at Jiwa', while ours
Roamed rugged Hazn, Samman and Mutathallim[11]

May God preserve you, vestiges of long ago: how sad
And desolate you've grown, since Umm al-Haitham left!

She moved off to a hostile land, and has since become
Inaccessible to the likes of me, Oh daughter of Makhram![12]

---

10 Many editors include, after this, two or three rather vapid lines that
    seem to me out of character with 'Antara's terse style, as well as
    illogical, as they describe 'Abla's physical attributes before the poet
    has even got to her campsite, the classic trigger for the reminiscences
    that follow. I think they were added later by someone who did not
    understand the first line's subtle literary criticism!

11 These place-names are now unknown; however, they do have
    meanings: Jiwa' where 'Abla lived meaning 'valleys', while his people
    dwelt in three places all having the connotation of 'rugged'. The
    loved-one's superior social status is a recurring theme in early poetry
    as well as later (as in Ibn Zaidun's eleventh-century 'Ode in the letter
    nun': see *Andalus* in this Poetry of Place series, Eland Publishing,
    2007).

12 Or Mahzam: one dot makes the difference, the textual tradition is
    undecided.

I loved her without thinking, while warring with her tribe,
And killing them: how daft, by God, to think of marriage then!

You are the only person I honour as my beloved –
Please don't ever think I could falsely tell you this!

How could we even meet, with her folk at Unaizatain,
When ours has settled at Ghaylam, with their foes?[13]

Although you resolved to leave and separate us thus,
The night your mounts were bridled was a dark and gloomy one.

I was surprised to see her family's baggage-camels eating dry
And thorny *khimkhim*-leaves, in the middle of the camp;[14]

Their milch-camels were forty-two, each of them as black
As the under-wing-feathers of the jet-black crow.

You can't help falling victim to those sharp, white little teeth –
Sweet to kiss and delicious-tasting as they are

Their scent as though a spice-merchant's perfumed pouch
Sent forth its fragrance to you, instead of her sweet mouth;

Or like an ungrazed meadow, green and grassy from the rain
With hardly any dung or marks of hooves.

Graced by the first pure showers from every cloud of rain,
Scattering puddles like bright silver *dirhams*,

---

13 It is clear from this line (which does not mention 'foes') that the
contrast of the two place-names would have struck the reader like 'I
am a Capulet and she a Montagu'.

14 *Khimkhim* are thorny, sticky little plants that are not satisfying to
camels, and if eaten reduce milk-production; a sign that summer is
coming, time to leave the relatively settled life at winter pasture and
seek other grazing.

Their waters pouring forth and gushing with every evening rain
Running freely over the surface, not dammed up.

The only being there was a solitary fly, humming
All the while, like a drunkard singing to himself

As he hums, he rubs one leg against the other –
Like a one-armed man bent on striking fire from a flint.

She reclines on a well-stuffed cushion, all morning and all night,
While I spend the night on the high back of a black, well-
      bridled mare,

No cushion for me, save my sturdy-legged mare's saddle
Full where I kick her, noble in her girth.

Do you think a Shadani she-camel could take me to her place,
One cursed with a dried-up, milkless udder,[15]

Proudly strutting and lashing with her tail,
Pads pounding through the sandy mounds we cross?

You'd think I was riding not a camel, but an ostrich –
Earless, with hummock-breaking, close-together feet,

One which the ostrich chicks flock to, like a herd
Of Yemeni camels called by a gibberish-speaking foreigner;

They follow the top of its head, as if it were a howdah
Or a funeral convoy, its burden shrouded like a tent –

---

[15] There are two variants here: the camel has a (naturally) withered
udder, as here; or it has been deliberately ablated, which makes her
run faster. It seems to me that in the latter case the poet would have
no cause to complain as he seems to be doing here.

A small-headed thing, coming back to its eggs at Dhu-l 'Ushaira
Like a fur-coat-wearing palace slave with ears cut off.

My camel drank water at Duhradain, then turned away,
Disgusted, from the stagnant pools of Daylam;

She shied off to the right, as though she was fleeing
Some big-headed beast that screamed at her in the dusk –

A cat, running right beside her, and every time she struck at it
Its claws and teeth put fear into her heart –

Endless travelling has given her a back strong as stone,
Firmly buttressed up like a well-pitched tent.

Even if you cover up with a veil when I'm around,
Don't forget I give short shrift to armoured men of war!

You should rather praise me for what you know of me –
For I've a gentle nature, if you don't harass me;

But if I'm treated badly, my wrath is terrible,
As bitter to the taste as desert colocynth.[16]

In the afternoon, once the midday heat is done
I've drunk my share of finest wine from brightly polished bowls,

In yellow, incised glass goblets, of a set
With the luminous, stoppered flagon on its right.

And while I may squander all my money with this drinking,
My honour stays intact, abundant, never blemished.

---

16 The colocynth plant may not be a household word in English, but the
two main words for it in Arabic ('alqam and hanzal) pop up all the
time in poetry as synonyms for 'bitter'.

And when I'm sober again, I'm no less generous –
You know well my character, how very noble I am.

Many's the rich beauty's husband I have slain, left
Lying, hissing heart's blood like a harelip's whistle

My hands struck first, with a swifter blow than his –
Thrusting sword met by crimson spray.

Have you never asked the horsemen, O daughter of Malik?
If you're really ignorant about such things –

They'll tell you I'm always in the saddle of a strong-swimming
        mount,
Suffering attacks and wounds from men in full armour;

First shying to avoid a spear-thrust, and then flying
Fearless to the massed archers' tight-strung bows –

Let them tell you, who saw the fight that day, how I'm
In the thick of battle, but stand back from plunder-time.

Full many an armoured warrior the others feared to fight, one
Not rushing to seek safety in surrender or in flight,

To him my palms were generous with their swiftness as they
        thrust
A seasoned, strengthened, truly straightened spear –

And with that sturdy lance, split his body-armour,
For nobility or rank is no protection from the spear.

And I left him as carrion for the lions to devour,
Gnawing his comely fingers, chewing on his wrists.

How many coats of mail did I rip asunder with my sword,
Worn by a famous warrior, fighting for his right?

His hands were swift enough, that winter, at the gaming-table;
Tore down the wine-shop sign, and was soundly blamed.

When he saw me dismounted, bent on fighting him,
He bared his back-teeth, but it wasn't in a smile!

I jabbed him with my spear, and then set upon him
With my true-edged sword, razor-sharp and India-made;

And in the midday sun, after meeting with me,
His head and fingers looked dyed with indigo.[17]

Oh antelope, fair game for those who have the right,
A right denied to me, I wish it were not so!

I told my slave-girl, 'Now you go and scout around,
And find out news of what she does, and report it back to me';

She went, and said 'I saw the enemies off their guard:
The antelope is easy prey for a skilful shot like you –

And when she turns her head, her throat's a young gazelle's,
Pure and fine, with a spot on its upper lip.'

(…)

I have heeded well my uncle's battlefield advice,
While lips revealed the mouth's white snarl,

In the throes of combat, where the heroes' only cry
Of complaint – as they die – is a wordless groan,

When the spears were pointed at me, I held back, but not
Through fear, there was no room to move.

---

[17] Spilt blood darkens quickly in the midday sun.

I saw them, massed together, urging each other on,
Coming at me – I charged them, a charge beyond reproach,

' 'Antara!' they jeered, their lances coming at us,
White ropes into the well of my mare's jet-black breast

I pushed her to attack them, and her white-blazened throat
And breast were soon all cloaked with blood;

She shied away from the spears as they struck her breast,
And complained to me, crying and whinnying –

Had she been able to converse, she'd have lodged a protest,
And would have addressed me, had she the power of speech;

But my own soul was cured, its sickness sent away
By the horsemen shouting: 'Come on, forward, 'Antara!'

The scowling horses charged across the sandy soil,
Long-bodied horses, mares and stallions both.

My riding-camels, docile, well-tamed, spurred by my firm
command,
They carry me – and my heart – wherever I wish to go.

My only fear was that I might die without War having turned
Her wheel against Damdam's two sons!

The ones who curse my honour, though I never insulted them,
Who – when I am not around! – swear they'll spill my blood:

No wonder that they do so, since I left their father
Carrion for scavengers and every old vulture!

Abd al-Masih ibn 'Asala

He was a Christian pre-Islamic poet (his name means 'Slave or Servant of the Messiah'), about whom very little is known except that he was of the tribe of Bakr ibn Wa'il (Shaiban) in Iraq.

Oh Ka'b! Why can't you mind your manners when you drink
    with us,
Behave yourself, and refrain from doing harm?

The day may be cloudy, but we take delight in songs,
And go to sleep like Persians, with melodies in our ears;

You, too, could wake up sober – but in true Namiri form,
You imagine she's the cousin of the brightest stars above:

And Ka'b must be restrained when she whacks him
On the forehead with that fat little wrist of hers!

And leaves his forehead streaked with blood,
Like a grape-harvester's fingers' crimson stain.

Wine is no brother to you, nor to those like you
Who think you can control yourselves no matter what:

It distorts judgement, makes fools of you
As soon as its heady vapours do their work.

Murra is my tribe, and when my mighty pen wounds you,
That wound is one you'll never staunch for good.[18]

---

18 There is an untranslatable play on words between the two meanings of the root *k-l-m*: to speak, and to wound …

'Umar ibn Abi Rabi'a

'Umar was from the Prophet's own tribe of Quraish, born
into a wealthy family of Meccan merchants. He was for a
time governor of a town in Yemen, but seems to have cared
more about wine and women and poetry than politics; he
died in 719 AD at the ripe old age of nearly eighty. He is justly
famed for his love-poetry, and was among the first to detach
the love-poem from its former place as but one section of a
long ode that also dwelt on camels, war, travelling and the
praise of the rich and powerful. In his urbane hands it
became something we would recognise today, a discrete
piece about his (real or otherwise) passion for a real person.

If only Hind had kept her word, and healed my soul
Of the misery it suffers from!

And just this once followed her own heart, unlike
Those flimsy souls who follow others' will.

The rumour says she asked her friends, at the bath that day,
As she stood naked, ready for a dip:

'Tell me truly, do you see me as he describes me?
Or does he overdo his praise?'

But they laughed all at once, and told her this:
'You think every eye sees the one you love as fair!'

It was out of envy that they told her that,
And envy's been around since the beginning!

She's a fresh young thing, and when she smiles,
Teeth white as camomile, or hailstones you can see.

Her eyes so black, their whites so white,[19]
Her neck is soft and supple.

She's tender, always cool when outside it's hot,
Even in midsummer's fiery blaze;

But in the winter she is warm, a young man's
Perfect blanket, when icy cold curls 'round.

I'll not forget the first time we spoke together,
With bitter tears coursing down my cheek,

I asked her: 'Who are you?', and she said to me:
'I am someone passion's wasted, sorrow's worn away.

We are the tribe of Khaif, the people of Mina –
For those we slay, there's no revenge exacted!'[20]

I said: 'Welcome to you, my heart's desire!
Now say your name – ' and she said: 'I am Hind!

My heart is grief-demolished, but there dwells within
A slim and straight young man in lovely robes.'

I said 'Your folks and mine are neighbours,
Close relations, kith and kin!'

They say she cast a spell on me, and if that is true,
How wonderful, how excellent a spell it surely is!

---

19 There is a single Arabic word for 'eyes of which the pupils are
    intensely black and the whites bright white', *hawar*.
20 We are in Muslim times now: Mina is the hill near Mecca where the
    final stage of the pilgrimage begins and ends, with the sacrifice of a
    sheep on the Eid al-Adha. The point is that killing there is sanctioned,
    even if the departed dies of love.

But every time I ask her: 'When's our rendezvous?'
Hind just laughs and says: 'Day after tomorrow!'

Who hides his sickness from the eyes of men? I'll tell
Zaynab what's on his mind and makes him anxious.

I'll tell any doctor who thinks he can cure me: just bring
Zaynab, here, you'll find what you're feeling for.

And if you can't cure me with *that* medicine,
I'll despair forever of doctors and their art!

I'll never sleep a wink at home, sitting up all night
On her account, until the earth covers up my head.

The full moon has risen to light my solitude,
While the night-watchman wandered from his post.

But I never took from her anything that's not allowed,
Only that we both dressed ourselves in rosy robes … [21]

We spent our time in innocent togetherness,
Not at all like the lies the envious spy spread wide.

Oh, how wonderful, wonderful, wonderful –
A lover who made me suffer, and I let him!

How wonderful are his white and pointy teeth –
If the night gets too dark, he'll gleam it away!

[21] This is obscure, perhaps a personal note that only Zaynab would
understand.

Farazdaq

Tammam ibn Ghalib Abu Firas, nicknamed *al-farazdaq* or 'the lump of dough', was born in Eastern Arabia sometime after 640 AD, and died at Basra in 730 AD. He wrote biting satires that often got him in serious trouble with the authorities. His poetry is an example of the old, relatively authentic tribal poetry that flourished before Arab culture became definitively urban.

Ziyad tempted me with his bounty, and I wasn't coy;
Why should I be, he's such a noble man?

If Ziyad wants to be generous, there are around him
Crowds of paupers with hands outstretched.

His doorway's rife with the seemingly needy,
The really poor, and some ambitious souls –

But finally I was afraid that what I took from him
Would conjure black and twisted thoughts among that
        motley gang;

I was compelled to seek refuge, as others were before,
In a night-journey to safety, across the wilderness.

At my leisure, I'm serenaded by ivory-engendered music
Coaxed by the unfurrowed wrist of a fragrant girl,

A pale beauty from Medina, born to ease and joy
Who never knew want or followed an outcast man;

She mentioned Ziyad's name, and spoiled my mood;
Skittish around me in her dyed Yemeni dress.

'Leave Ziyad out of this!' I told her, 'For I see
Death's dark pit yawning every place I look.'

By my life, a *bedu* girl around whose tent
The wind blows freely front and back,

Is dearer to me than your overslender pearly maid,
Who breaks into a sweat if she but puts down her fan.

I swear, Nuwar's gone to the dogs, driven
To ruin by her mind's flighty dreams;[22]

She followed the advice of her cousins, and ended up
On a camel's hump with the open desert for a guide.

Nuwar refused to allow me what other wives
Freely gave before – but she'll not get off so light;

Even though a certain man is taking her side, beware!
That's like fighting lions with a stick –

---

22 Nawar was the poet's wife, by all accounts a banshee who nearly
drove him mad while they were married; once divorced, he looked
back fondly on his time with her ...

It's fine to have courage when safe behind a door,
But in a fight your stick may end up shorter than their paws!

The Commander of the Faithful knows what he's about,
Applying the Prophet's strictures to his humble flock –

I'll put my faith in you, good Ibn Zubayr, but know
That she's a sorceress, melting stones with her talk;

And nobody snags the sympathy of the crowd
Like a brazen angry wife who's crossed her husband.

I repented as had a famous one before,
Who broke his bow – when Nuwar left me, divorced!

Even though I kept my cool, in hand and heart alike,
It was a conflict with both destiny and free will.

She was my Paradise, and I left her
As Adam, gone blind, left the Garden;

And I was left like one who gouged out his own two eyes,
And found that in the morning, no sun shone down on him.

Jarir of Kulaib-Tamim

Jarir is the great competitor of Farazdaq, and the question of which of the two was the better poet was such a burning controversy during their heyday that endless anecdotes tell of their verbal jousting and the fights of their respective partisans. They are both Umayyad poets, dying around 728 AD. Arabs of noble lineage, proud of their desert heritage, they wrote in the mainstream style of their time but began the move away from conventional *qasidas* (odes) to the *qit'a* or circumstantial piece.

Passion led me down the path of Mawiya's love,
And its guidance did not lead me far astray;

I love to see the hills, and am drawn down to the valleys
For love, Abd Qais my friend, roams high and low.

Moved, I ask him: 'Abd Qais my friend, where in all this
World, do you think love most kindles and blazes up?'

He said, 'I think it blazes fiercest on the soil where grow
The bitter absinth and the thorny *gharqad*-tree.'

When I'm poor I live on nothing, and when I'm rich, I waste;
I'm quick to take my leave when I tire of a place.

Fast off the mark, I have no fear of death
When my fingers clench tight around my sword's hilt:

The sword that cuts right through to the bone,
And whose dire blow outdoes even my tongue!

Those eyes, those eyes that carry affliction in their gaze,
They slay me, then refuse to give back my life.

They keep attacking my heart until it's paralysed –
Though they're the weakest things of God's creation.

And you, you merely watched while the pupil of my eye
Drowned – for did you ever see a pupil leave its eye?[23]

I'd give my soul for one I dearly love to flee,
The one whose presence is disaster;

The one who's never there when I wake up,
But visits me when sleepers slumber deep.

---

[23] An untranslatable play on words: *insan* means both 'pupil of the eye'
and 'person, man' …

Bashshar ibn Burd

This important poet lived from about 714–83 AD, that is to say he was active during both Umayyad and Abbasid times, not to mention the transition from an Arab and Muslim world ruled from Damascus by Arabs to one ruled from Baghdad by, for the most part, non-Arab Muslim converts or their sons. Being the son of a Persian freedman, he was doubly representative of the new Abbasid spirit which gradually turned away from the preoccupation with Arabic tribal issues and the desert generally.

He is chiefly known for his love poems, which are a curious mixture of clichés and colourful detail. The last poem of his in this series is a forceful diatribe against the old Arab hegemony in politics and verse, praising the nobility of his own Persian lineage. Towards the end of his life (no coincidence), he got on the wrong side of the Wazir of the Caliph al-Mahdi, was executed and thrown into the Tigris.

No one but you knows why my longing grows so fierce,
And why a grieving heart like mine throbs, and throbs.

Whenever I hear your name, my passion blazes up,
And the thought of you brings salt tears to my eyes.

At night I lie, my eyes hostage to tears,
To wake with yearning heart, sad and dejected.

When I'm in society, with talking all about,
I sit bowed down as though a stranger in their midst.

They say: 'A *jinn* has cast a love-spell on his heart!'
But a gazelle reared in luxury caused my grief.

Whenever the South Wind gently blows, it stirs
My passion for you, and I am overcome.

My friend prefers the North Wind, when it blows,
But the South Wind is far dearer to my soul –

The reason's simple: when it blows, it wafts
To me a hint of charming Abdah's scent.

Abdah is the only cure for what afflicts me,
My only doctor, however much she hides it.

As fragrant as the perfumer's flask, and more:
She's gentle if I chide her, sweet as sweet.

Abda's love has taken sole possession of my heart:
The heart I'll never share with anyone but her.

For God's sake, don't be cruel enough to slay
A lover who sighs and weeps for you all night!

He is cut off, estranged from kith and kin:
The only family tie he has is love for you.

When we're apart, I dream of fortune's favours,
But you cheat me of my dream when next we meet.

By God, I cannot fathom whether Abdah will reject
My love, or whether it will find its just reward;

How miserable I am! My love grows strong and tall,
While the soil that nurtures it is waste and desert land.

She even tells me: 'If you die pursuing passion,
You'll be burdened with the sin of suicide –

Repent while yet you can, for I fear that God
Will not look kindly on you when you come before him.'

That's what she advises me, now that I've gone grey;
While others ask my counsel – seems I'm a man to trust;

So I just told her: 'In loving you I've done no wrong,
Or sinned at all: what is there to repent?'

As you know, we're neighbours, pass in public all the time,
But strange as it may seem! Never one-on-one;

I'd love to know if only once I'll visit you alone,
Little Abdah! Without any spies around,

Our hearts would find respite from the fever of our passion –
For the lover has no hope for cure except the one he loves.

If ever I forget one of the things Fate brings down on our heads,
Of all the sundry things that happen here below –

It won't be the taste of your mouth,[24] of which I drank –
No, not even at the sunset of my days.

I only live for the nourishment you give me, as though
I were an exile from my tribe and all their wealth;

I might tell you I'd forget you for an hour or two of sleep,
But for you my fears and sorrows would still be plain to see.

---

[24] Literally, 'taste of your saliva'; two aesthetic particularities of Arabic
love-poetry are that the saliva of the beloved, rather than the kiss, are
usually celebrated; and the beauty of the mouth resides in the teeth
of which smallness, whiteness and tidiness are sung about more than
the lips or mouth itself.

Wine-stewards of mine, come both – pour me a drink,
One laced with the saliva[25] of a lovely, tender girl:

I suffer from thirst, and the only cure for that
Is a sip from the freshness of a certain maid's cool lips.

Her smile is white as daisy-petals, her voice
Trills like embroidery, adorning the finest robe;

She has taken her place in my heart's inner core,
And has conquered more than the most covetous ever could.

She finally told me, 'I'll meet you in a night or two,'
And as the nights go by, they wear out all that's new –

She delays our meeting, while I'm beset by sighs,
The kind that eat away your heart, be it made of iron.

Greetings to you, old campsite at Dhu Tandhub,
By Shatt Hawdha and the slough of Qa'nab;

Let riders stop a while – no, not just for a while,
Let them stay and give up riding altogether![26]

Some hearty types there are, who shy away from drink,
Refusing so much as medicine for scorpion-stings;

Fair maidens leave them cold, and morning's first light
Never found them weeping over a lover's former home.

25 See the preceding footnote.
26 The poet is alluding ironically to the traditional practice of mentioning
   lots of obscure desert place-names in the 'romantic' prelude to the
   full-blown Ode.

I've softened up the sourpuss ways of even such a one,
With the sweetness of my demeanour, without the need for
        force;

By and by, when passion finally took its hold on us,
And he let himself relax and play the game,

I opened up my heart to him, and told him all there was
To know about Su'da, and all about Zaynab –

And all the while, as I told him this, my eye
Welled up with tears, I was moved without respite;

The Dwelling and its former folk have all long gone away,
But that which dwells within my heart will abide forever.

The place we dwell in is a marvel in itself,
Where tawny lions roam, and oryx herds alike;

Back when Su'da lived here, along with all her tribe,
That was the life, a life of wondrous ease and joy!

Since then, hard times have ground us down, after those
That were anything but hard to bear –

Those same hard times have snatched away Su'da and her tribe,
And nothing's left but memories of her, and her tender love.

And when my companion became my confidant,
He asked about my love for her – I told him this:

My friend, you don't need to ask about my love:
Just look at my body, you'll be quite amazed;

You'll see the wasted frame – measure it if you doubt –
Of one who travelled through her heart, but did not take root.

I pine for Su'da, imagine her near me when I sleep;
But she's not, she's far away, untouchable.

She's a girl of Mecca, if she goes out of town,
It's to the gentle sands of Na'man, or those of Mughrib;

I'm all hung up on a mere illusion of her, a dream –
If only it were real, and not a dream at all!

'Umar blamed me on account of the girl I love,
(I do hate those who blame others for no cause) –

'Give her up!' 'No!' I said; he replied 'You must!
The rumours about you two are all over town!'

I said 'Why should I make excuses, just because rumours run?
Anyway those people will not excuse me anything!

I will not hide my love for the one who slays me,
No, no, and no again! I hate the tales they tell,

But you can blame me all you want, soon it'll be too late;
I'll soon, the good Lord knows! be at death's door;

Be off with you, then, and tell them I'll have none of it,
I won't wise up, as they would say, the Devil take their souls!'

What could any of their lot possibly say to this, a passion
That Destiny has nurtured until it's fully ripe?

Listen, folks, I have nothing in common with them,
Those arrogant fault-finders – of others' faults,

Making such a weird, weird quarrel out of this – may the mouths
Of those who blame a lover be choked up with stones!

No true believing Muslim ever blamed a man for love,
So to Hell with them, they're infidels!

We love each other, and it's enough for us
To see each other, and to talk a while,

With maybe a little kiss, no harm in that –
Provided I don't undo my clothes!

But when the curtain's closed across the door,
I might slip my hand to feel inside her dress;

Or leave a little love-bite on her arm,
While my arm bears the mark of hers;

And her anklet-bells flash and jingle on her leg,
And the sound of panting breath grows louder still;

The lovely creature's hand droops coyly down,
And she lets drop a tear and says: 'Stop, oh stop!

And go away, you're not at all like I had heard –
You're a wild one to contend with, by the Lord!

My nursemaid's out today, I'm left alone with you –
There's no one but God to be my guide with you:

Dear God! Take my side, you see how weak I am,
From this wanton's roving hand (and he's not even drunk!)

He's such a strong, rough fellow, he's impossible to stop –
He squeezed me so tight, my bangle got all bent!

And then he rubs his beard, all black and grizzly too,
Against me, pricking me like needles do.

He overwhelmed me, seeing my family were away –
They would have been ashamed, if they'd been around!

I swear by God you'd not have escaped alive –
Now go! You brutal vicious bully you!

What will my mother say when she sees my bruised lip?
What will you do when this story gets around?

What, what ever will my nursemaid think of me?!
If only prudent caution had been of use to me today!

I knew that you would do just what I feared –
So what do you have to say for yourself, you brute?'

On hearing this, I told her 'Take it easy, my pet!
For I've got vast experience and know what it's about:

Just tell them that a bug with claws attacked you!'
(as though some bugs actually have claws!)

Who will be the messenger,
Who will tell all the Arabs for me,[27]

Both the ones that live today,
And those who're sleeping in the ground,

That I am descended and come from a noble line,
The noblest lineage of any in the world?

---

27 This is propaganda: a Muslim of Persian origin making fun of the
Arabs, the godless ways of the Umayyads and the rustic mores of the
bedu. When Bashshar says 'we' are kings, he means the Persian race
and the new Abbasid dynasty writ large, for he obviously was no king.
He also exaggerates a bit as the Abbasid armies never got close to
Tangier.

My glorious grandfather was King Chosroes,
And my father was none other than Sassan;

Great Caesar was my uncle, if you care
To trace my family tree back that far.

How many – yes, how many! ancestors of mine
Wore a crown upon their noble brow?

Haughty they were, seated in counsel,
With all other knees duly bowed;

He comes to his court of a morning
Clothed in brilliant jewels,

Wrapped in splendid ermine,
Standing aloof, on a curtained dais;

His servants hasten to him,
Bringing golden goblets,

Never did he drink watery milk
From goatskins, or eat from leathern bowls;

My father never sang a camel-driver's song
Trailing behind a mangy camel!

He never went to get a bitter colocynth,
Cutting it open out of sheer hunger;[28]

Nor did he ever go up to a desert mimosa,
Shaking its branches with a stick in hopes of food;

[28] Compare this sneering reference to the marginally edible colocynth,
with those in Arab poets like Shanfara or 'Antara, who boast of their
ability to survive in the desert, eating colocynth and drinking fetid
water.

And we certainly never roasted a scaly skink,
Its tail twitching in the fire!

I never had to dig the stony ground for lizards,
In fact I never ate such things at all!

Nor did my father warm himself,
Straddling the campfire's flames,

Oh no! nor did he ever
Ride upon a wooden camel-saddle,

For we are kings and always were,
Since the beginning of recorded time;

It was we who summoned horsemen
From Balkh, to tell the truth,

And brought them to water in the Aleppo streams,
For no one ambushes us;

Until, victorious, they trampled
The hard ground of Syria

And then drove on to Egypt, amid
The noise and tumult of our multitudinous host.

And added Egypt's realm to the one
We had seized before;

Our cavalry pushed onwards
To Tangier the marvellous,

And restored its sovereignty
To the Arab Prophet's kin;

For who could oppose the Guide and his
True Religion, without losing all?

Who has ever rebelled against it,
Or opposed it, and was not plundered?

If we are wrathful, it's a noble wrath,
On behalf of Islam and God Himself!

We are the bearers of crowns,
And the awful might of monarchy.

Abu-l 'Atahiya

Isma'il ibn al-Qasim lived at Kufa and Baghdad and died in
about 825 AD. His early poetry was mostly about wine and
love, his later production being ascetic and pious.

Alas, how short was the time we spent
Between Khawarnaq and Sadir!

We dwelled in chambers of godly Paradise,
And swam in a sea of bliss;

We were like falcons, a band of youths
Who grasped the very reins of Time's steed –

Each of us was bold in matters of love,
Not shy or backward in the least.

We passed around the crimson wine,
The cream of its vintage it was;

It was a virgin, nurtured by the sun's rays
Through the burning mid-day heat,

Never coming near the fire, not tainted
With the cooking-pot's foul grease.

Here's to a tunic-robed one, passing back
And forth before the crowd, shy as a fawn –

In his hand a glass, one able to draw out
The secrets from your inner mind,

A glass as bright as the pearly star
In the hand that passed it around,

Leaving the noble guest unable to tell
What is coming from what is going;

Slender maidens came to visit us,
Fresh from resting in their rooms;

With plump buttocks, and rings
Dangling from their waists;

Their faces are bright, through their veils,
Averting their glances, dark-eyed –

Blissful, coddled creatures all,
Anointed with fragrant ambergris;

Sweeping along in robes of beauty,
With their undergarments, and silk.

They never see the sun, except
Like an ear-ring, glimpsed through curtain-gaps;

And so to God's steward we resort,
Fleeing from the stumbler, Time.

We tired out our mounts, in haste to be with him,
Travelling by morning and by night;

Their cheeks were drawn with effort, and it was
As though they had the wings of eagles,

Cloaked in darkness, dashing over plain
And rugged hill –

Until at last they brought us to
The lord of cities and palaces,

Who was mature as the gravest elder,
Even before he was weaned!

AL-HAMASA

This is not a poet, but an anthology of poems arranged by theme, including (but fortunately not restricted to) 'boasting' or 'pride' poems (*hamasa*). The chief merit of this collection is that it was made by the great Abbasid poet Abu Tammam himself, and we thus get an impression of what he considered the worthwhile verse of his time and earlier, a somewhat surprising choice as many of the poets cited are now considered minor at best. The following eight poems are chosen from the 'love poetry' (*nasib*) section of the *Hamasa*.

Al-Simma ibn 'Abdullah

You may well pine for Raya, but it was you who left
And moved away from where her kinsmen lived.

It's all your fault – you wanted this, and now
You feel the pain of loss at your own hand.

So friends, say farewell to Najd, and those who dwell at Hima;
Saying goodbye to Najd may not seem much to us,

But I'd sell my soul for this land and its hilly charms,
So pleasant in summer, and in spring as well.

Those evenings spent in Najd will never come again
To you, so let your eyes fall to weeping –

When I saw lofty Bishr in the distant haze,
Longing seized my soul, and anguish

Brought tears to my left eye. When I sought to check it
For its bad behaviour, they both poured forth at once.

I kept turning towards her former home,
Until my neck got sore all round,

And when I remember the days we spent together at Hima,
I bend a bit to ease my heart, for fear that it might break.

Abu Sakhr al-Hudhali

I swear by Him who makes us weep and laugh,
The bringer of life and death, whose word is our command:

When she left me, I became jealous of wild creatures,
Seeing how peacefully they pair, untroubled by fear.

I wish that every night, love made my passion grow –
Even if satisfaction must await the end of time;

I marvel that Destiny tried so hard to thwart our love,
And when our love died, Destiny calmed down.

But even now, the moment I set eyes on her,
My mind goes blank and I quite lose my wits.

Ibn Udhainah

You say your passion for her has cooled? You know
She was born to be your love, as you were to be hers!

She is fair-skinned spawn of soft luxury, subtly
Making her so slender, yet so roundly formed;

She greeted me, but only coyly – as I told my friend,
How great it was in spite of being so small!

If she was feeling pangs of guilt at the prospect of dalliance,
I'd use my mind as envoy to her heart, and assuage them.

Kuthayyir

Kuthayyir ibn 'Abd ar-Rahman was a Shi'ite poet at the
Umayyad court, who celebrated his beloved 'Azza so
fervently that he is known as 'Kuthayyir 'Azza'. He died in
about 723 AD.

It amazes me, 'Azza, but I'm finally cured of you,
After living for so long in such a deathly state.

If a soul that's finally cured can be said to find repose,
Then I must be cured, as this is a kind of peace;

My head may have lost its former covering, but
My heart is still bound tight, burdened as before.

Anonymous

In dead of night, Zaynab came knocking at my door:
'Welcome', says I, 'has time long past returned?'

She said: 'Stay clear of me and don't even come close';
But how could I avoid you when it's you I need the most?

They say 'Can one still play around when one is over thirty?'
I say: 'Can anyone play around who has not yet reached that age?

Going grey would be dire indeed, if at the first grey hair
A man was no longer left to have a little fun!'

Hafs al-'Ulaimi

I tell my better judgement not to thwart my falling in love,
And to my grey hair I say: 'Don't frighten lovelies away!'

I sought – and found – passion's pleasures, low and high,
And chased both kinds of love, until I had enough;

But now I beseech you, God: if you won't let me have Qadhur,
Don't let that fellow have her, take her to you as she is;

And if God really won't let her and me unite,
Then may He sunder every other loving pair!

Ibn at-Tathriya

I'm asking such a small thing, a single glance from you –
As though anything that comes from you is small!

Oh companion of my soul, you who are my only friend,
The purest and best friend I could have;

I hid my love for you to spite our enemy,
And put no faith in any meddler;

Is there no place on earth for my lonely complaint, where
I can tell the fear I feel – and is there no hope to meet?

I worship you, but my enemies are many, and I'm far
From home – and here, there is no one to take my side.

I used to call on you on some pretext or other,
But all pretexts are exhausted, what is left to say?

I haven't got a reason to come your way,
And can't send you my messenger every day.

I've filled pages with my complaints, folded double –
Some day they'll be published, and they are long!

You really should refrain from causing my death – you're
            too weak
To bear the burden of my murder, come Judgement Day!

Ibn al-Dumaina

Can it be, Oh God's creation! That I can neither come nor go
Without being followed around by some loathsome spy?

Can it be that when I visit you, either by myself
Or in a crowd, I'm looked on with suspicion?

What's suspicious about it, when a well-born girl
Sighs for her noble lover, or he pines away for her?

As for that sandy hillock not far from where you live,
Even if I avoid it now, it's the dearest place to me;

By God, I'll stay true to you so long as you are to me,
And I'll be grateful for the smallest grace you show me.

I'll take the favours that you freely grant, and reverently
Turn my back on everything you disapprove of.

Please don't destroy the remnants of my poor soul,
For you know, yearning for you has all but done it in!

I feel all flustered when I think of you, as though
Your very absence from me was itself a spy!

Qays ibn al-Mulawwah (Majnun Layla)

This early Umayyad-era poet of the Bani 'Amir is less famous for anything he did than for what was done after him: his constant passion for Layla, beautifully attested to in his poetry, was embroidered on after his death and a whole cycle of romances grew up, in Arabic but also in Persian and Turkish, that was widely popular for a thousand years. Very little is actually known about him and some commentators have expressed doubt that he actually existed. One is tempted not to worry, and to say that 'if it was not he, it was someone else of the same name' … A poet who, as a child, fell in love with a child named Layla and wrote beautiful, chaste ('udhri, after the Banu 'Udhra who were famous for celebrating a sort of Platonic love in their verses) poems about his unrequited love for her.

People say, 'you could be cured of her if you wish',
And so I tell them: 'I don't wish!'

How could I? Love for her is what sustains my heart,
Like the rope that brings the bucket from the well.

Her love has taken root within my breast; there
It grows, and will endure no matter how oppressed.

I am blamed most cuttingly for this, and in the heat
Of reproach and blame I suffer grievously.

They ask: 'Who is she anyway, and wherever does she live?'
I say: 'She is the sun, the heaven's her abode.'

They sneer: 'Whoever heard of loving the sun itself?'
And I just answer, 'Fate has sentenced me to this.'

Once Fate has decreed its verdict on me,
Only Fate can cancel that decree.

Abu Nuwas

Abu Nuwas ('He of the Dangling Locks') Ibn Hani Al-
Hakami was born in Ahwaz in about 762 AD and died
around 814 AD. He was well-educated, studying at Kufa
and spending time with the bedu to perfect his Arabic. He
was in and out of favour with the grandees of his time
including Harun al-Rashid himself, spending some time
in prison. Abu Nuwas wrote much of his poetry during
the reign of Muhammad al-Amin, Harun al-Rashid's son
who inherited the throne at the age of twenty-two. Amin
('steward', 'trustworthy') was a libertine and former pupil
of the poet. Abu Nuwas knew as much about poetry as
anyone alive, being said to have memorised the *diwans* or
collected works of fifty women poets, which is saying a lot
(perhaps too much), as we do not even have evidence for
the existence of that many. He was a famous drinker and
libertine and, though he wrote some *zuhd* or ascetic poetry,
his heart was not in it.

It was in his wine poetry (*khamriyyat*) and love poetry
written to both men and women, that he left us a memorial
of world-class standing. To be able to read Abu Nuwas in
the original is itself justification for the rigours of learning
Arabic! For at last with Abu Nuwas, we have left behind
the artificial mooning over abandoned campsites – except

sarcastically – and are face-to-face (for so it seems, his poems are so vivid and original) with a flesh-and-blood, highly erudite rogue with a lust for life, a sense of humour and no truck with fools, hypocrites or bigots.

I have included a relatively large number of his poems, with an example or two of all the genres, to show the breadth of his virtuosity. I have not included any of his really obscene satires, less because of an aversion to such things than because the obscurity of the vocabulary makes me unsure at times just what is going on, physiologically. The classification of his poems has a random character, some being about both love and wine, for instance; one should ignore this.

Encomia (praise poems or madh)[29]

Greetings and welcome, Oh most excellent Imam
You were created as the Caliphate's purest gem –

Oh Amin of God, may He protect you while you're home,
And watch over you whenever you venture abroad;

For the whole Earth is abode to you, and God
Is your companion wherever you are.

You are so like the Prophet in gracious generosity,
And like unto al-Mansur in your manner and your way.

[29] I include these encomia as examples of the genre, but they are not his best work. Al-Mansur was the founder of the Abbasid dynasty and of Baghdad.

70

The fullest of Night's moons sailed out upon the Dolphin[30]
Riding the flood, steadfast on the swell;

The Tigris was illumined by its light,
Both banks of the river shone for joy:

My eye never beheld such a wonderful ship,
Splendid under way, splendid at the quay –

When its oars propel it forward, it races
Through the water, and then sedately coasts.

God destined it especially for Amin, who was
Created to be crowned with the diadem of kings.

Oh you of the pretty face, with a mole on your silky cheek,
Be generous – even with the kind of scraps a miser gives:

I'll take even the smallest favour,
Since from small ones big ones grow;

God and al-Fadhl's opinion saved me
From the bonds and chains of prison;

He freed me from Fate's oppression,
Just when I had despaired of rescue.

Have you forsaken me, oh Ja'far ibn Abi Fadhl?
Upon whom can I rely, if even you forsake me?

---

30 The name of one of the Caliph's ships, apparently of Greek origin
(like his shipbuilders).

To whose high station can I appeal, to whom of all men,
If you won't help me – you, al-Fadhl's brother?

Tell Abu 'Abbas (even if I am a sinner) –
For you are most worthy to receive his favour;

But don't ruin the affection it took twenty years to build,
And don't spoil the graciousness of favours past.

Love-poems (nasib)

I have not differentiated between heterosexual and other poems, as it is impossible to be sure in every case; there was also a convention of using masculine gender for clearly female lovers, as evidenced by references to clothing or anatomical detail.

She had these words engraved on the stone of her ring:
'He whose lover tires of him, has forsaken sleep'

And so I had my own ring graven thus:
'He who sleeps is stupid compared to the wakeful man'

So she had it erased and wrote this back to me:
'He who really loves neither sleeps nor stays awake'

I erased this in turn, and wrote back to her:
'By God, I am the first corpse to go pale from grief'

Which she erased, and wrote back to counter me:
'By God, I never spoke a word to him!'

She was a palace-girl, and I loved her at first sight,
With the love of chaste 'Urwa the 'Udhri, or the Madman
of Najd.[31]

But when she played hard to get, I said: 'Give in!'
She said: 'With a face like that, how could I love you?'

I answered: 'If there were faces in the souk
For sale, and all it took was cash,

I'd change my face and buy a nice new one;
Maybe then you'd give yourself to me!

But even ugly as I am, I am a poet, don't you know?'
She said: 'Not even were you the Bard himself!'[32]

Some pretend that I've reformed, but if only they knew!
My inclination's towards any graceful, doe-eyed fragrant one;

How to reform, when my heart is split in two, between
Glancing eyes and the sheen of wine in the cup?

If I turned back to piety, I'd be schizophrenic:
Pulled between my rich life-style, and going broke!

Luxuriating, carousing: over time it wears you out;
Real hardship is getting satisfaction from the one I love.

---

31 This reference (just 'the Najdi lover' in the original) is probably to
    Qays ibn al-Mulawwah, known as Majnun Layla (the 'Madman for
    Layla'), see above.
32 The Bard referred to is al-Nabigha adh-Dhubyani, one of the authors
    of a *mu'allaqa* (see the Introduction).

There is no virtue in life, except in plenteous wine
Amid roses, and violets, and myrtle;

Listening to a singer sing, while cups are proffered
To us, then a fifth one, and a sixth!

Oh, you who would re-kindle your dying fire,
You can light it any time from the brands of my heart!

And here's to a *saqi*, who just like the moon,
Sweeps away the darkness from the sky;[33]

When I told him what I desired of him,
His grace shed grace all around:

'Come to me and listen, you'll hear wondrous things –
Marvels old and newly wrought alike!'

He bent down, my mouth came near his ear,
Closer than the two ear-ring holes they bore.

They were kissed from front and back,
Like the very first garden of blooming youth;

What can drinkers or carousers know,
About a broken heart which revels in its woe!

---

33 a *saqi* is of course a cup-bearer, wine-pourer, courtesan, general object
of pleasure and desire; of either or indeterminate gender.

By the truth of your faith, the religion from Nazareth,[34]
By the Messiah, and Luke, and by John the Baptist,
By the bishops as they bow before the Patriarch,
By the Apostles atop the monastery church,
By the Gospels and Scripture in the hand of the priest,
By the Psalms, chanted rapid-fire,
By the monasteries and all who live therein –
Won't you take pity on my piteous laments
On account of that seductive gaze of yours?

The one who is so miserly with paper,
Deserted me after we'd been close;

He called me to prayer – and to despair in love,
Sorely trying my heart at being thus deprived;

Like a champion of the holy House of Hashim, who,
When he staked his claim, saw his 'Abbas snatched away![35]

We had a rowdy drinking bout, he and I, and each
Man of our company was the very ornament of society.

When they drank, their *Sunna* or tradition was:
Whoever turned away a cup, to pour it on his head!

And others, when they drank, would not leave
Enough to drown an ant's egg in their cup!

---

34 Abu Nuwas wrote a series of love-poems to a young Christian boy
    named 'Abd Yashu', even using Syriac words in some of them.
35 The Abbasids traced their line to Abu al-'Abbas, an uncle of the
    Prophet Muhammad and like him, belonging to the tribe of Hashim.

Oh, what a fresh and fragrant apple
My lover used to sweeten his breath!

His natural sweetness made it more fragrant still,
And perfumed the whole assembly with it –

And so the cup was sweet – and the wine-jug too,
At the place where its lip was kissed by his cup.

Oh Night, you are not over –
Oh Morning, you have not come!

Oh Night, if you sought your way,
Then you have gone astray.

My love! For what fault must I
Suffer your avoidance thus?

I swear by God I never left you,
So stay as I wanted you to be;

By God! I swear I never cut you off,
When you were close, or from afar.

I tried my best to get over you, and
Just look what happened to me –

Now see what I wished for,
Just look at what I wanted!

Drinking songs (khamriyyat)

Once again I guided the mounts of my trusty friends
To a wine-seller's house, arriving at midday –

And when the guardian of the place spoke, we knew he was
No Muslim: we thought well of him, and he ill of us;[36]

We asked: 'Are you of the religion of the Messiah,
Son of Mary?' He turned away with muttered curses,

For he was a Jew, of they who love you outwardly,
But in their inner hearts think only to betray you.

We asked his name; he said: 'Samaw'al, though I'm better
          known
As "Abu – Father – of 'Amr", but there isn't any 'Amr;

The Arab nickname brings me no honour, nor
Does it increase my glory or my pride –

But it's lighter to pronounce, shorter to boot,
And less awkward to say than many others.'

We were taken aback at the sharpness of his tongue, and said:
'Most excellent man, Abu 'Amr, now give us wine!'

He turned his back, as though averse to us, his
Shifty eyes looking us up and down,

Then said: 'By my life, were you of my faith, I'd blame
You for carousing, but as it is I excuse you.'

---

36 They thought well (he was breaking no rule of his religion), he ill (he
    knew they were breaking theirs).

The wine he brought was unctuous gold, and all
We could do was prostrate ourselves before its majesty.

By the time we left, it was past three, but the wine was so
very good
We could easily have devoted a month to it;

A bunch of rascals as has never been seen before!
And I was mixed up with them to the hilt.

Now, when prayer-time comes round, you'll see them
rushing through,
To finish before their drunkenness dissipates.

How many gazelles like unto so many moons,
Sweeping the gloomy darkness from the town!

I asked him for love, generous love, but he
Was miserly and gave me none at all;

So I told that fawn who was playing hard to get:
'Oh sweet of soul (and just as sweet of body),

How many fellows did you grant your love to,
Without ever getting pregnant or giving birth?'

He answered: 'You're trying to make me pity you –
But the gazelle does not have pity on the lion!'

I said: 'Come, let's get some of that stuff
The infidels put on a pedestal and baptise!

Daughter of the vine I mean, when decanted
With pure spring water will splash you with its froth!

Until the two of us will take ourselves away
To where no spying eyes or jealous one can see.'

I poured the winy nectar down his throat
And did not stop until he could no more;

I came up and undid his clothes, and then
Laid out his thigh with my hand;

Then embraced him, and stayed wrapped up in him
And his mouth, like a shower of hail.

He rose when his drunkenness was past,
Allied to sadness, grieving passionately.

Two lovers who had veiled their faces,
We came up to the Black Stone[37] to kiss it;

We were absolved without having sinned
As though we had come there by appointment!

If the crowd had not pushed us, we'd
Not have recovered from it until the end of time.

We both kept our faces veiled,
But on the side, with our hands,

We did in the mosque what no
Innocent person ever did in a mosque.

[37] The Holy of Holies in the *Ka'ba* at Mecca. This is a very daring verse.

Oh twin of my soul, from my tribe of al-Hakam,
You ignored my suffering, as I tossed and turned –

So pour me some of that vintage wine,
That ripened to old age while in the womb.

Desires of youth stirred within her, after
She had reached the age of senility;

She was created for the day she'll be mixed,
Though she's Time's companion from days long past;

She stood before the people like an actor,
And told them histories of all the nations.

A hand created for the pen and the cup
Mixed her, and that calmed down her ardour some,

In the company of noble youths, who knew
How to take their pleasures head-on.

Then she flowed through their veins,
As an antidote flows through a sickness.

When she was mixed, she lit up the house
As morning lights up night's gloom –

And a traveller, lost in the night, could follow her
As a caravan is guided by a landmark.

Leave old abandoned campsites to those who would
      weep there,
And spend your time instead on wine and
      drunkenness!

Drink your fill of golden, ruddy liquid,
Until your night confuses with the day

Daughter of ten summers, she's seen
No fire except that of the sun

She slumbers still in the deep pit
Of a wine-jug stopped with tar;

Then comes the mixing, with a necklace
Of bubbles dancing round,

As though it were strung with pearls,
Little pearls alongside bigger ones.

Whenever it catches your eye
As it passes round and round,

You glimpse the decorations on the cup,
Little pictures of jackals, etched on its sides.

From the hands of a charming cupbearer,
His livery stamped with beauty itself

Attending in turn to each party-goer,
Dressed in a cloak of wine –

And those who drink too deeply
Find the wine's crimson in their eyes!

The singer's there, and as usual,
Sings and gestures gracefully

Voices rising mingled, stirring
The heart with memories.

My friend, can you see a trace of such a fire
In Asma's abandoned campsite?

Go, tell that fellow standing there, weeping over ruins:
What would it hurt, if he just sat down?[38]

Leave aside Salma and her tribe's old dwelling, and instead
Take a morning-drink of Karkh's fiery wine,

The daughter of Time, forgotten in her jug –
Until cleansed of every speck of impurity,

Like heart's-blood. Whenever a drinker tastes of her,
She'll make him scowl and frown all right!

Satire or invective (hija')

Praise be to God for this wonder of wonders!
Haitham ibn 'Adiy has turned into an Arab!

Oh Haitham ibn 'Adiy, you're no Arab!
Nor one of the tribe of Tay', except by constraint,

---

38 The poet is satirising the ancient practice of weeping over abandoned
campsites, which often began: 'Stand a while, my two friends, and
weep with me/ At the vestiges of my love's former dwelling …' Salma
was a name used in several such passages.

You claim to be descended from the Bani Thu'al –
So put the letter *dal* before the *'ain* in your pedigree![39]

I can just imagine you, atop a bridge, riding
A noble steed with a family tree just as noble as yours;

And I can see you've armoured him in pus
Instead of rough palm-leaves and rugged stuff.

You're a fine one, with no family worthy of the name –
Unless you sought a borrowed lineage from next door;

You're (as you always were) busy with your intrigues
With the non-Arabs – and, when it suits you, with the
      Arabs.

Ali and his friends spent the night
In shame, mostly on account of

A fawn-like creature who hardly bored them,
Since they joined his ears to his heels!

He did not fear his Lord in the holy month of fasting –
Oh Lord! Thou shouldst not forgive his sins!

---

[39] Untranslatable: if you invert the two letters mentioned in the name
'Adiy, you get *da'iy*, 'impostor'. Sigh!

Khasib's bread is made from celestial flour
He defends it with might and main;

He has turned food into fruit forbidden to hungry
People, but lawful to those who have plenty.

If the hungry ones saw that loaf of his, they would rejoice
As a fasting man at the evening call to prayer.[40]

Sa'id treats his loaf of bread as equal to himself,
Turning it over, and playing with it in turn –

Pulling it from his sleeve, he sniffs at it;
Then puts it in his lap, and talks to it.

But if a poor man comes and begs his share,
Having just lost his mother and closest kin,

Sa'id attacks him, whips him all around,
Breaks his legs, and rips out his moustache.

The Court is shrouded in grief
Since Ibn Kaba went away

Oh raven, omen of separation and bad luck,
Measure of the stain of sin –

You bill of divorce,
News of mournful calamity,

[40] That is, they get joy from seeing the loaf, like the joy of hearing the
prayer-call that ends their fast for the day; that is, virtual joy.

Paradigm of stress and woe,
Agonies of dire misery!

Oh, loaf rejected by the grocer,
Dry and hard as stone:

What was that solemn face
With which you greeted me today?

And that from but a scribe,
One who's passing unfamiliar with the pen.

Khasib's soul is entirely made of lies,
His prattle causes trouble for those who listen;

His very robe weeps that its coat-tails
Should be swept to and fro by such a dog.

Razzin[41] brought forth her brood from her anus,
And in the eyes of each, an evil sign;

Half-blind boys and girls, groping for their way,
And one-eyed ones, liars all and ugly.

The things I've said about you will endure to the end of Time;
While everything that you have ever said, is – wind.

41 Razzin was the mother of Isma'il ibn Naibakht, someone the poet
   was not fond of.

Jokes and riddles

Today, I swore by the lute
And by the dice, and backgammon,

And by wine-drinking
Near the narcissus and the rose;

I swore by hunting, with the falcon
And the hawk, with dogs and leopards;

You did spur on my heart to this,
Lord of my heart, so earnestly –

But I cannot stop myself
Showing you how fond I am.

I did a spot of divination, when I got your letter –
Divination by auspices and omens of birds;

I saw that it was strung together with
A lute-string, and sealed with pitch;

I said: 'Its back is pied just like the cloak
That singing-girls wear, and in their style;

The lute-string points to a musician,
And the sealing-clay to a wine-jar' –

I've come to you with heartfelt joy,
And made no mistake about the house!

What do you think of my powers of divination –
Am I not one of the greatest of philosophers?

When my lover grew cold towards me,
And cut me off from letters or even news of him,

My anguish grew until I almost died from
Remembering him, fretting and thinking;

I called on the Devil, and said to him privily,
With tears coursing down my cheeks,

'Don't you see what agony I'm in, how my eyelids
Are sore from weeping and sleeplessness?

If you have not made my lover love me –
And I know that's within your power,

I never composed a poem, nor listened to a song,
And never felt the heady wine working within me;

I never stop studying the Quran
And reciting pious sentences,

And keep the holy fast of Ramadhan
And my only goal in life is doing good.'

The clock had hardly struck three times after that
When my lover came to me, and apologised …

People told me: 'Go and wash, it's noon
Prayer time'; but I was having a drink,

And said half-heartedly: 'I will';
They replied: 'Skipping prayer is a serious sin!'

I said: 'More serious still is this:
A tender fawn will slip away,

If I leave now – he won't wait for me,
And happiness will desert me!

Prayer is not for the likes of me,
My wickedness is famous –

So save your breath, but don't blame me,
Anyway, I do have an excuse:

If I need to wash because of what I'm doing,
Doing it with him is purification, not defilement!'[42]

Elegy

Your tears poured forth like a flood
On hearing of the death of Waliba;

When Abu Usama died, a mournful
Dirge rose up from the town.

The tribe of Bani Asad was sorely stricken,
And the Bani Nizar frowned their lament

For him who was their spokesman,
And their leader in momentous times.

---

[42] Literally: 'If I have a *janaba* ('ritual impurity such as caused by having had sex, requiring one to wash before praying'), well, *janaba* from the one who caused mine is itself purification.'

Don't leave us, Abu Usama!
But Destiny is implacable,

Sending mortal arrows to
Snatch us all away.

It is written that obliteration awaits us,
Religion or no, and we must all go that way;

How many brothers have you left
Worn out by sadness on your account!

With you alive, it was hard to see
Any misfortune as a calamity!

By your life, Death has left us nothing at all
To cheer us on the morning of sadness;

But I feel as though I cheated Death, in a son
Who died: no old age or senility awaits him.

Complaint

If I go on being broke like this,
My friends and brothers will avoid me;

I'll have to sell my clothes, and even if I do,
I'll still be caught between the house and the door!

I was amazed, though life is full of wrinkles
And Fate brings us marvels of many colours,

By a friend who – after being my now and my hereafter,
Attacked me in public as fiercely as a wolf!

I was utterly blameless, I deserved no such rebuff;
He revealed his vile hypocrisy – and I had loved him so!

My only one among all of humankind,
How could you curse and censure me like that?

I thought of a proverb (if only I followed it!)
Coined by a winning talker, no loser at all:

'Don't praise a man until you've tried him out –
Nor should you ever blame him without a trial.'

The Lord be praised! Is there no end
To the trials of Man by Man?

Love is the kernel of the soul, but
I've found poverty degrading;

I watched silently as Fate did what it did,
But then Fate came and shat upon my head.

Abu Firas

Al-Harith ibn Sa'id ibn Hamdan was born, probably in Mosul, in about 314 AH (926 AD). He came from a long line of warriors and poets, and his mother was a Byzantine captive named Sakhina. He was a noble of the House of Hamdan, whose father Abu-l 'Ala fell under suspicion of treason, for which (suspicion, not treason) he was murdered by his nephew, Abu Firas' cousin, Hassan, after the latter succeeded to the emirate on the death of his father Abu-l Hayja.

Abu Firas was raised by his cousin 'Ali and given an excellent education. 'Ali rendered notable services to the Abbasid rulers in Baghdad, and was given the title *Saif ad-Dawla* ('Sword of the State'). He went on to conquer northern Syria and found his own dynasty at Aleppo, in the front line of the Islamic–Byzantine confrontation. Abu Firas was given responsibility very early and distinguished himself as a soldier, later being wounded and taken captive when surprised by a large detachment of *Rum* (Byzantines) while out hunting. He wrote some of his best poetry during his years in prison, while waiting to be ransomed. He was killed in the strife that followed 'Ali's death, apparently while trying to seize power himself.

The great poet Mutanabbi visited the court at Aleppo while Abu Firas was there, and this may have encouraged the young man in his own vocation. His poetry is personal, written in simple and direct language, and clearly speaks from the heart; a sort of red-blooded Arab Wordsworth, except that with him we feel we are in the presence of a lusty soldier with an uncharacteristically sensitive heart and no tolerance for fools. He was also famously handsome.

She was a virgin, honoured by her family, but
The swords of our horsemen showed her no honour.[43]

She became engaged by the sword-blade, and married
Against her will: her dowry part of the common loot.

She found her master, ready to be wed, giving
Thanks to God – but for *her* family, it was a funeral.

Some of my fellow-tribesmen tried to reach the heights
After seeing that was where my ambition led me;

Their efforts at greatness were laboured,
Constrained as poetry is by metre.

Even better than a venerable wine, served
From the hand of a tunic-clad, mincing fawn,

Is the clash of arms in battle's midst,
Staining the earth with dark heart's-blood.

---

43 This sympathetic description of a Byzantine captive may have been
inspired by the poet's beloved mother…

We wrapped ourselves in garments of the night,
Until the infant head of Night began turning white.

We slept like twin branches of a sapling, teased
By the north and south winds of the morning.

The way we were would send the envious off in fury,
And the Watcher's eye would turn away from us –

Until the morning's first light appeared, like
White hairs peeking out beneath dyed side-whiskers!

Oh Night, you left us without our scolding you;
You, Morning, were most unwelcome when you came.

How splendid is his face, ravishing me with its down –
A petal of Nisrin roses on the page of his cheek.

That which covers his cheek did not sprout from within,
But is the essence of his coal-black, curly hair.

He drives me to distraction with his saliva
And his new beard: wine on pearls, musk on roses.

News came to me of you,
Secret things about you –

I saw in them signs and traces,
All saying: you forgot me.

Coming from you, I saw them
With my heart, a visceral seeing;

Once Love grows cold, even
Fire cannot revive it.

May Aleppo be bathed in plenty, so long as you are there:
Full moon, life-giving rain, fulsome spring!

If I leave, my soul resides there still, and I do leave
So heart-heavy my young steed can hardly walk.

If her master's heart were not so sorely tried,
My mare would have no worry in the world.

The whole earth and its cities seem deserted as I pass,
Every single place abandoned by life and love –

I feel like one who throws stones towards the sky;
As high as they go up, they're sure to fall back down.

I never had a sorrow that did not abate with time,
And as each fades a new desire comes in its place;

That's why even if I'm complaining of his love
I still voice my desires, louder than my complaints.

I cannot live without him, nor with this passion – don't
        they say:
'God never burdens a soul with more than it can bear'?

The day I realised that the more I hear
People blame you – the more I love you,

Right then I wished that for evermore
No mortal would do anything but blame you!

Fate has two sides to it: one firm, the other slippery;
Life has two tastes, bitter colocynth and honey.

And Time's the same – so when they're riding high,
Wise men don't swagger, nor despair when times are tough.

Man would be truly happy if the good times were the rule,
But as it happens the bad ones last every bit as long.

We fear life's trials, but they don't last forever; while
The happiness we long for passes soon away.

So don't grieve over passing worries, nor exult
Over happy days destined to disappear.

Some people, though, are greedy for happiness,
Not losing hope until the time of woe is nigh.

Mortal though he is, man is full of desires – in the grip
Of ever-growing covetousness and hope.

Abu Firas had a sure touch with all the genres of poetry, if he was not above a bit of dilettantishness or triteness in his love-poetry. But it is in the poems written from his Byzantine prison, from which his cousin 'Ali (Saif al-Dawla) was famously slow to ransom him – despite having in his own custody a member of the Byzantine royal family – that he left his mark. I shall let them speak for themselves …

> If I am 'visiting' Kharshana as a captive,
> How often have I been here as a conqueror!
>
> I watched as houses were burned down,
> Palaces destroyed by the flames –
>
> And saw captives being brought to us,
> Black slaves and dark-eyed beauties;
>
> We would choose for ourselves the slender,
> Supple maids, the young and tender fawns.
>
> If my night is long up on these hills of yours,
> I've also been – briefly – happy here;
>
> With you I found sadness, to be sure,
> But with you I also found some joy.
>
> If I've been victim of events,
> I'm determined to suffer patiently:
>
> Through patience it may be that God will
> Enable this place to be conquered easily.
>
> Men of my sort are one of two things:
> Captives, or rulers!

Those of our line inhabit only
Thrones, or graves.

Coo, little dove, perched on my prison window-sill[44] –
Can you, little neighbour, can you know what I feel?

Not knowing what it is to love, you never tasted
Separation's pain, nor did cares weigh upon your mind.

If only a heart oppressed by sadness
Could take wing, and fly way up on high!

Come, come little dove, Fate's not been fair;
Come close to me and share my suffering.

Come and you will see how weak my soul's become,
Wavering in a tortured body, all worn out.

When will the captive laugh, the free woman weep,
The wretch keep silent, the leisured one mourn?

My eyes have more reason than yours to weep;
But my tears, despite what happened, I'll sell dear.

---

44 In the original, the verse starts with *'aqúlu wa qad náhat bi-qúrbi
hamámatun'*, the first word ('as I speak') sounds like a dove cooing.

Oh King, you who train
Your robes on glory's ground,

Spring has come with all its charms,
Impregnating the clouds with its pearls;

Lovers' eyes are awed by its beauty,
Rivalling the loved one's cheeks.

The wine is poured, but tastes
Flat and insipid, with you far away.

Hardly had Fate exiled me here,
Than voices began saying: 'Who is this Harith anyway?'

Exile makes me recall those promises of his,
Promises that have turned to threadbare rags!

It's not my fault, was never my desire,
That I am not a sworn ally of yours;

Now if you forget me, know that while I live
I'll never stop thinking of you: I'll not forget.

Do what you wish, I'll remain – though far away –
The one who comforts, one who shares.

Feast-day, you've come round again, but your comfort is cold
For the one who's heart is battered and tormented.

You've come again, to meet the gaze of one
Whose eyes are veiled from all your joy.

How desolate is the house whose master wakes up,
In the degrading livery of a servant!

To those of such a house, the feast-day seems
Devoid of all beauty, deserted by joy;

I wonder what is happening to me: Fate and all its works
Conspire to deal me supernatural blows!

What's wrong with the stars in the sky, are they distracted,
Stuck in their constellations – is their fate like mine? [45]

I spent all night watching them – until morning broke,
Wandering aimlessly, as though they'd lost their way;

But don't you see how they lean down towards me?
You'd think they pitied me, and were on the brink of tears.

[45] 'Constellation' and 'tower' are the same word in Arabic (*burj*); not an
original image, but it is especially apt in the case of Abu Firas, writing
while imprisoned in a tower.

Alas! Mother of the captive, may you be blessed[46] –
I know how hateful were the captive's woes to you.

Alas! Mother of the captive, may you be blessed –
He is struck dumb, unable to stand or walk.

Alas! Mother of the captive, may you be blessed –
Who will the herald run to tell, when my ransom's paid?

Alas! Mother of the captive, may you be blessed –
Whose locks, whose hair will be smoothed, with you dead?

When your son journeys abroad, by land or sea,
Whose protection will he seek, to whom will he appeal?

Sweet sleep would be a blasphemy for him,
And feeling any joy, a sacrilege.

You've had to taste agony and death,
With no son, no relative at your side;

Your heart's beloved may have been absent
From that place, but all the angels of Heaven were there.

Let every day you fasted weep for you,
Patiently fasting through the mid-day heat!

Let every night you rose to pray weep for you,
Rising as the day began to break!

Let every poor oppressed soul you protected weep for you,
When few took pity, none would help at all!

---

46 Literally, 'may the rain-clouds water you'; I think the closest equivalent is 'may you be blessed', as a literal translation of the Arabic does not convey what he meant. He wrote this poem from prison, on learning of his mother's death.

Oh Mother! What long anguish you knew,
With no one at your side to help!

Oh Mother! How many secrets deep inside
Your breast, have died unrevealed with you?

Oh Mother! How many times was news of my return
Brought to you, that I would soon be there?

To whom can I complain? To whom can I appeal,
When my breast is too narrow to contain it all?

Which woman's prayer of entreaty will shield me?
Whose bright face will shed its light upon me?

Who will guide me past mortal dangers, who
Will help me out of the worst situations?

Losing you, my only consolation is that I shall soon
Follow you to where you've gone.

Al-Mutanabbi

Abu at-Tayyib Ahmad Ibn al-Husain 'al-Mutanabbi' ('the would-be prophet') was born in al-Kufa, in Iraq, in 915 AD. He was of economically humble stock (his father may have been a water-carrier) but they traced their descent from a Yemeni tribe, the Bani Jufi. The boy received an excellent education in the Arabic language (spending a year among the bedu), and at some point got mixed up in the religious controversies of the day, including a Shiite conspiracy where his involvement earned him his nickname. This unsuccessful and dangerous experience behind him, he gave up politics and spent the rest of his life becoming, and being, a poet.

He spent part of his career at the Aleppo court of Saif ad-Dawla (Abu Firas's cousin), but that was not wildly successful and he seems to have left at dead of night. He ended up in Cairo at the court of a former Nubian slave named Kafur ('camphor'). Again, things turned sour and our poet fled in disarray, launching biting satires back at the patron he formerly eulogised. A few years later he was returning from a trip to Persia when he was attacked and slain by bedu brigands.

Al-Mutanabbi was highly controversial while he was alive (mainly because of his political dabblings), and after his death. It became almost fashionable to draw up lists of the passages he had plagiarised from earlier poets as well as general departures from sound religion and good manners. This spiteful practice – not really justified – may have been in part inspired by his humble origins. Among the literate public, however, his fame increased and he is probably the most quoted and studied of all Arab poets. For my taste he is (with occasional exceptions) too precious and pretentious, too bombastic and humourless to rank as a favourite along with 'Antara, Abu Nuwas, Abu Firas or the great poets of Muslim Spain. But he must be included given his stature, as well as the fact that after him, the quality of Arabic poetic creation declined drastically, some would say never to recover. Whether this is even partly true and why it might be if so, is beyond the scope of this little anthology; but how could one help but be at least partly won over by a poet capable of writing the oft-quoted verses:

For the horsemen and the night and the desert all know me,
As do the sword and the lance, the paper and the pen

Lines composed extemporaneously in his youth

How high can I go? what challenge shall I fear?
For everything God created, and all that he did not,
Is as little to my ambition as a single hair on my head.

To Saif ad-Dawla on his recovery from an illness

You are saved! And with you glory, nobility as well;
From you, your pain is visited on your enemies.

Raids against the infidel are restored, healthy again, like
    you –
This restores joy to noble deeds, and showers of blessings
    pouring down.

The sun recovered its former light, which it had all but lost,
As though its body had grown sick, its visage pale.

Lightning flashed forth at me, from your kingly cheeks:
Without your smile, bounteous rain can never fall.

He is called the Scimitar, but not because they're alike –
For how could the master resemble the servant?

He distinguishes the race of Arabs by being one of them,
While foreigners bask in the sun of his munificence.

God has bestowed His help for Islam above all,
Even though all nations share in His bounty;

It is not only you I congratulate for getting well:
When you are safe and sound, so are we all.

Panegyric to Kafur

Not just sickness, Death itself is done for – if you call it a
       healer;
And Doom itself is doomed if you but wish it so:

And that you did, when you desired to see a true friend,
And there was none – or rather an enemy, pretending.

If it had pleased you then to live in humiliation,
You should not have readied your Yemeni scimitar!

Nor should you hold out your lance, ready for the raid,
Nor seek the help of a swift, full-grown mount.

Shyness is no good to lions when they're hungry,
They're only feared when hunting, on the prowl.

I loved you, heart of mine, before you loved the one who
      left;
If he has proved a traitor, let you be faithful still.

Separation, I know, makes you complain after him,
But you are not my heart, if I see you complain!

Tears flowing from eyes betray their owners,
Even if they flow for faithless ones.

If generosity is not bestowed free from injury,
Then praise is unearned, and wealth does not last.

Each man's soul has character traits that show
You if he's really generous, or just pretending.

Be still, oh longing of my heart, for perchance
Your sincere love is for one who loves you not!

You were made to have a loving nature – if you could but
      go back
To youth again, you'd weep from pain of leaving age behind.

But there is a sea in al-Fustat, one I've visited on my life,
My sincerity, my love – and my rhymes.

How many short-haired horses did we ride, lances forward
Between their ears, which they followed through the night?

Moving ahead on unshod feet that struck the stony ground
Leaving behind a graven image of the breasts of falcons;

Black-eyed gaze through the pitch-black night,
Knowingly picking out distant dim shapes,

Ears pricking up at the slightest muffled whisper,
As though reading a man's secret inner thoughts;

Straining against the reins held by the morning riders,
As though those reins on their necks were snakes.

Resolutely riding goes the body in the saddle,
As though its heart were travelling on its own;

All seeking Kafur: forsaking all the rest, for he
Who seeks the ocean despises petty streams.

(…)

Satire on Kafur composed the day before the poet fled from Egypt

Feast-day! What kind of feast-day is this?
Is this a relic of the past – or an evil omen of what's to be?

The ones I love are far across the desert from me; if only
That same desert was between you and me instead, and yet
      another one!

If I'd never sought to reach such heights, neither my strong
      she-camel
Nor my long-bodied mare would have brought me,

And I'd have shared my couch not with my sword, but
With (far sweeter!) slim and refined young beauties;

Time has worn out my heart and my liver, so that
There's nothing left to be enslaved by eye or neck.[47]

And so, *saqi*s, is that wine in your two cups?
Or are they full of worry and insomnia?

I must be a rock! For I am not moved at all
By this wine, or by these lovely songs!

---

[47] The liver was held to be the seat of emotions, along with the heart.

When I wanted wine, crimson and pure, I found
It only when I'd lost the one my heart most loved!

What has been my portion of this world? The strangest
Thing, is that I'm envied for that which makes me weep!

I have become a wealthy man, in treasure and in possessions;
And if I'm rich, my wealth is nought but promises.

For I have ended up among these liars, who deny their guest
Due treatment while he's with them, honoured leaving when
      he goes.

Men have hands and tongues to be generous with – I wish
That they had none at all, and they themselves did not exist!

Death would not come to seize the soul of any one of them,
Without a stick in his hands, such is their stench.

Hanging from their swollen belly is a limp, ragged strap,
So they cannot be counted among women, nor among men.

Every time a wicked slave murders his master,
Or betrays him, must he have been trained in Egypt?

The eunuch has become leader of the runaway slaves –
The free man is enslaved; the slave must be obeyed.

In Egypt, the gardeners sleep while the foxes eat their fill,
And still the ripe grape-clusters are not gone;

The slave can never be a brother to a pious free man,
Even when the slave was born in a free man's clothes.

Never buy a slave without a stick to go with him,
For slaves are unclean, nearly useless creatures.

I never thought I'd live to see the day when a dog
Would do me harm and be praised for it!

I never imagined that the race of men would perish,
While the likes of His Gracious Whiteness [48] would exist!

Nor that that black man with a ring in his lip
Would be obeyed by that bunch of flunky cowards.

Hungry he is, and eats of what I've got; he holds me here
So that I call him 'Great and Mighty', and 'Much-desired'.

Any man who is under the heel of a pregnant slave
Is oppressed, bleary-eyed and faint of heart.

What a woeful situation – woe upon him who accepted it!
For fleeing such disaster long-necked Mahri camels were
          created;

When this happens Death tastes sweet to him who drinks it,
And annihilation is delicious to one who's been reviled.

Who do you suppose taught the eunuch Negro to be noble –
The white tribe he comes from, or his 'royal' sires?

Was it his ear, bleeding from the slaver's blows? Or his
Real worth, being left unsold when offered for a penny?

Kafurello is so base, he almost deserves to be excused
For being so – but some excuses are themselves reproach!

The explanation's simple: if white stallions can do no good,
How do you expect black eunuchs to do so?

<hr />

[48] This is another untranslatable pun: literally 'father of whiteness',
meaning 'giver of bounty', both meanings meant ironically when
applied to Kafur; and secondarily meaning 'misfortune'.

Al-Hallaj

Al-Hallaj, the 'wool-carder' (al-Husayn ibn Mansur al-Hallaj) died in 922 AD. He was a Persian but wrote in Arabic, and is known for his *zuhdiyyat*, 'mystical or ascetic poems'. He was beheaded for his heresy, and his tomb at Baghdad became a pilgrimage destination. Other Abbasid poets before him had written in this genre, such as Abu al-'Atahiya (who was probably sincere) and even Abu Nuwas (who almost certainly wasn't). But Al-Hallaj brings into Arabic the personal, transcendental mysticism of divine love found in better-known poets such as Jalaleddin Rumi or – remarkably – Saint John of the Cross. Though he died before al-Mutanabbi, it is perhaps fitting to end this anthology on a note of pure love rather than the grasping intrigues of the court poet.

Peace, then silence, and then mute;
Knowledge, then passion and discovery

Clay, mixed with fire, mixed with light;
Cold, and shadow, then the sun.

Stony wasteland, then the plain – then the desert,
A river, then the sea; then dry land.

Drunk, then sober, then aroused;
Close, then together, then joy,

Embracing, then releasing and forgetting;
Separation, then union, then – consumed by fire.

Entranced, then returning, pulling back;
Revealing, then hiding, finally dressed as chosen one:

These are phrases whose meaning is reserved
For those to whom the world's not worth a farthing,

Voices behind the door; but well we know
That mortal conversation's empty noise.

The last images that visit the mystic mind
If he reaches his goal, are 'fate' and 'self',

For mortals are servants to their desires,
While the Truth of Truth, once found, is holy – only that.

There can be no separation between You and me, ever since[49]
I awakened to the fact that closeness and separation are the
      same;

If all forsake me, loneliness is my companion –
For how could I be lonely when love is all around!

All glory is Yours, creator of pure perfection;
Your lucid worshipper, I bow down to You alone.

---

[49] The first line of this poem contains four words derived from the
trilateral root *b'd*, basic meaning 'separation'; untranslatable, this
kind of word play enables Arabic poets to reinforce their message in
a way that would seem precious in a Western language.

When I think of You, I am convulsed with passion;
And when I forget You, with sadness and suffering.

My entire being has become hearts, yearning for You,
For the sickness of love – impatient for its pains.[50]

I loved Your love with all my all, my holy one!
You revealed Yourself to me, unto my very soul;

I turn my heart towards those that are not You,
And see only estrangement – but You, You are my joy;

For here am I, a prisoner of life, snared in men's society:
Oh, take me out, bring me to You, out of this sordid jail!

---

50 There is a (probably apocryphal) tradition that this quatrain was
composed by princely command at a banquet, and thus can be read
as ambiguously evoking both earthly and divine love.

INDEX OF FIRST LINES

News came to me of you 93
No one but you knows why my longing grows so fierce 49
Not just sickness, Death itself is done for – if you call it
    a healer 104

Oh, how wonderful, wonderful, wonderful 43
Oh Ka'b! Why can't you mind your manners when you 40
Oh King, you who train 98
Oh Night, you are not over 76
Oh twin of my soul, from my tribe of al-Hakam 80
Oh you of the pretty face, with a mole on your silky cheek 71
Once again I guided the mounts of my trusty friends 77

Passion led me down the path of Mawiya's love 47
Peace, then silence, and then mute 109
People say, 'you could be cured of her if you wish 68
People told me: 'Go and wash, it's noon 87
Praise be to God for this wonder of wonders! 82

Razzin brought forth her brood from her anus 85

Sa'id treats his loaf of bread as equal to himself 84
She had these words engraved on the stone of her ring 72
She was a palace-girl, and I loved her at first sight 73
She was a virgin, honoured by her family, but 92
Some of my fellow-tribesmen tried to reach the heights 92
Some pretend that I've reformed, but if only they knew! 73

The Court is shrouded in grief 84
The day I realised that the more I hear 95
The fullest of Night's moons sailed out upon the Dolphin 71
The Lord be praised! Is there no end 90
The one who is so miserly with paper 75
There can be no separation between You and me, ever since 110

Those eyes, those eyes that carry affliction in their gaze 48
Today, I swore by the lute 86
Two lovers who had veiled their faces 79

'Umar blamed me on account of the girl I love 54

We wrapped ourselves in garments of the night 93
What's wrong with the stars in the sky, are they distracted 99
When I think of You, I am convulsed with passion 111
When I'm poor I live on nothing, and when I'm rich, I waste 47
When my lover grew cold towards me 87
Who hides his sickness from the eyes of men? I'll tell 43
Who will be the messenger 56
Wine-stewards of mine, come both – pour me a drink 52

You are saved! And with you glory, nobility as well 103
You may well pine for Raya, but it was you who left 62
You say your passion for her has cooled? You know 64
Your tears poured forth like a flood 88

Ziyad tempted me with his bounty, and I wasn't coy 44

INDEX OF POETS